Metal Jewelry
Made Easy

Metal Jewelry
Made Easy

A Crafter's Guide to Fabricating
Necklaces, Earrings, Bracelets & More

Jan Loney

LARK BOOKS

A Division of Sterling Publishing Co., Inc.

New York / London

Prolific Impressions Production Staff:

Editor in Chief: Mickey Baskett
Graphics: Karen Turpin
Styling: Lenos Key
Photography: Jerry Mucklow
Administration: Jim Baskett
Indexing: Miche Baskett

Cover Design: Celia Naranjo

Library of Congress Cataloging-in-Publication Data

Loney, Jan.
  Metal jewelry made easy : a crafter's guide to fabricating necklaces, earrings, bracelets & more / Jan Loney.
      p. cm.
  Includes index.
  ISBN 978-1-60059-473-1 (hc-plc with jacket : alk. paper)
  1. Jewelry making. 2. Art metal-work. I. Title.
  TT212.P36 2009
  739.27--dc22
                                          2009003811

10 9 8 7 6 5 4 3 2 1

First Edition

Published by Lark Books, A Division of
Sterling Publishing Co., Inc.
387 Park Avenue South, New York, NY 10016

© 2009, Prolific Impressions

Distributed in Canada by Sterling Publishing,
c/o Canadian Manda Group, 165 Dufferin Street
Toronto, Ontario, Canada M6K 3H6

Distributed in the United Kingdom by GMC Distribution Services,
Castle Place, 166 High Street, Lewes, East Sussex, England BN7 1XU

Distributed in Australia by Capricorn Link (Australia) Pty Ltd.,
P.O. Box 704, Windsor, NSW 2756 Australia

If you have questions or comments about this book, please contact:
Lark Books
67 Broadway
Asheville, NC 28801
828-253-0467

Manufactured in China

ISBN 13: 978-1-60059-473-1

For information about custom editions, special sales, premium and corporate purchases, please contact Sterling Special Sales Department at 800-805-5489 or specialsales@sterlingpub.com.

About the Author

Jan Loney

Jan Loney is a metal artist in Pittsburgh, PA, a city steeped in the history of steel. Her work ranges in scope from site-specific installations to small-scale sculptural work and jewelry. Loney's designs and work vary from decorative to functional, and quite often embody both. She is the 1995 recipient of the Three Rivers Arts Festival Westinghouse Purchase Award and the 2002 recipient of the Marietta College Outstanding Young Alumna Award. She exhibits her work nationally.

Jan's interest in metal began in high school and has steadily increased in the twenty years since she began working in metal. Her start was creating raised hollow ware—taking a flat sheet of metal and hammering it into hollow forms without the use of seams or soldering. This helped to form her love of hammering metal and the delicate marks left by the hammers' blow. Jan now works in a variety of metals, enjoying the opportunities and challenges each presents.

Working as an artist-in-residence at various Pittsburgh area schools has allowed Jan to bring her artwork to students and serve as a role model to young aspiring artists. She has become skilled at teaching students to create jewelry and metalwork using limited resources and recycled materials. Jan says that "teaching gives back to me as much as I give to my students."

Visit Jan's website: www.metalier.com

Acknowledgements

Many people have helped me to this place in my life. My parents set the stage for my life and career as an artist and gave me the courage to pursue my creative spirit. My husband and children provide daily inspiration to continue creating new work. Thank you all for your love and support.

A Word from Jan

My work as a metalsmith is part art and part science. For me, art is the medium that combines different areas of learning—a synthesis of science, math, and history. In order to create patterns and shapes, I often utilize mathematic principles of geometry. To understand how metal moves, how it changes state while being worked or heated or rapidly quenched, I look to the science of metallurgy. When I choose to patina or oxidize metal, I fall back on chemistry and the reactions between various elements. I am drawn to patterns in nature, be they veins in leaves or the arrangement of a modern day fossilized snake skeleton. Traces such as hammer marks that recall the process of creation are often left in my finished work. I enjoy the challenge of abstract ideas being transformed into tangible objects and often compare the recognizable in uncommon surroundings.

Table of Contents

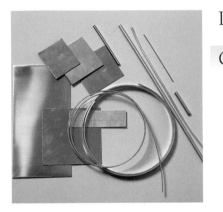

Polished Anticlastic Bracelet

Leaf Prints Collection

Reticulated Pendant

Introduction

A **smith**, or **metalsmith**, is a person involved in the shaping of metal objects.

Within this book you will be introduced to quite a few metal fabricating techniques. All of the techniques are within a beginner's realm of capability. First of all, some very easy *cold connecting* techniques will be described for making chains and bracelets. You can then progress to metal fabricating techniques of shape-cutting with a jeweler's saw, forging and forming the metal with a hammer, and using a torch to do *hot connecting*. This introduction to a variety of techniques will afford you enough familiarization with metal working methods to be able to choose a technique in which to concentrate and become proficient.

It is quite intriguing that something as hard and rough as a hammer could be one of the most essential tools in producing delicate and exquisite jewelry pieces. For centuries jewelers have referred to their craft as *metalsmithing*. The word *smith* (the archaic English word is *smite*) means "to hit" or "to strike"—and a hammer is the tool that is essential for this hitting and striking that forms fine metal into jewelry. During the process of learning the techniques of metalsmithing described in this book, you will learn the importance of the hammer in the creation of your jewelry pieces.

Precision and Repetition

Precision and repetition of the techniques are two of the most important aspects of successfully creating beautiful jewelry pieces. Whether playing sports, creating artwork, or performing surgery, doing something over and over will allow you time to examine the subtle nuances of those movements and procedures. Your jewelry-making skill will improve each time you repeat a technique.

When working with metal, consider the importance of each of your movements. As you are using a file, for instance, concentrate on how to hold the file to achieve the desired end result. Consider

These lightning bolt and cloud earrings, fabricated in gold and platinum, involve advanced techniques of cutting and forging.

how to push that file over the surface of the metal while making very fine adjustments in order to remove just enough metal to make a square corner. Adjust too much and the file will remove metal from an area that didn't need it; push too hard and the file will gouge out too much metal. All of this is able to be corrected with more metal and more time. However, repetition of your skills, and giving proper attention to each action will help you achieve satisfying results while saving time and money.

Embrace the areas of work that you don't particularly enjoy and learn the fine points of those tasks. Sawing used to be my nemesis so I looked for every possible way to avoid sawing. I learned there is no substitute for the jeweler's saw and saw blades in jewelry making. Now I attempt to saw as perfectly as possible. Accuracy in sawing means less time needed for filing which is the next step in jewelry making.

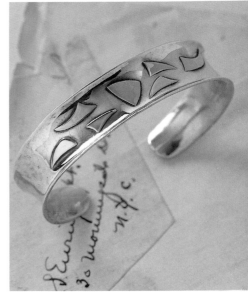

This silver bracelet has gold cutouts soldered onto it. Working with both gold and silver on a single piece of metal takes knowledge of how each metal type will respond to heat.

The Metalsmithing Process

As time goes on, my journey in creating art is all about the process; the product that I get is just an extra reward. There is so much more to the process of work and creativity that goes into a finished piece than can ever be conveyed in words to another person. In a way, everything that I have ever made in some way contributes to all the work that follows it. There are infinite tips and tricks and connections that have become so engrained in what I do that I may not even realize I am doing it.

Teaching for me is a natural extension of creating work. Conveying skills and processes to fresh minds is a way to refresh my vision and my path as I create new work. The creative mind is always searching for new solutions to the same problems and that is why I find teaching inspiring and vital to keep my own work fresh. Creativity will fuel your work; but remember to feed your creative soul as you would feed your body in order to stay in optimal health.

CHAPTER 1

Getting Started

This chapter will introduce you to the character-istics of the metal as well as instruct you on how to measure, mark, and work with the metal. Please read the important safety concerns outlined in this chapter.

Raw Materials

You can create jewelry from a variety of metal types including gold, copper, brass, and silver. In this book most of the fabrication is done with silver. Metal is also available in a variety of shapes and forms, from flat sheets to various shapes of wire, and casting grain metal. The metals that I worked with to make these projects are *nonferrous* metals, or those that do not contain iron, such as sterling silver, brass, copper, and gold.

Sheet Metal

Sheet metal is flat and is available in various gauges or thicknesses. It can also be purchased in flat shapes such as disks or squares. Choosing the correct gauge of sheet metal is important. It is important to use metal conservatively to avoid excess cost and weight, but not to such an extent as to jeopardize the quality or functionality of the jewelry.

Wire

Wire is most commonly round in cross section, but can also be available in other shapes such as square or rectangular. Half-round wire is available in low dome or high dome, and a few suppliers also make triangular wire. Other specialty shapes such as decorative gallery wire can also be found in catalogs. Wire is usually measured from 30 to 0-gauge. A search of a few suppliers will provide an array of materials with which to create your designs.

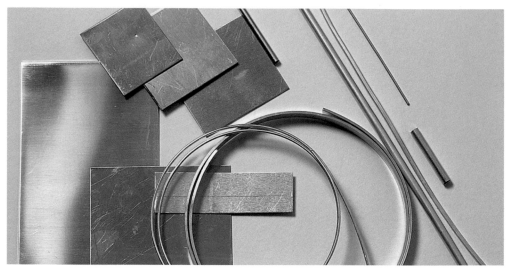

Types of Metals

Sterling Silver

Pure silver is much like pure gold in that they are both very soft and are usually alloyed to make them more functional for jewelry making. Sterling silver is 92.5% silver and 7.5% copper or other metal.

Coin Silver and Reticulation Silver

Coin silver and reticulation silver are generally alloys of 80 to 90% silver and 10 to 20% copper. The added copper is useful in the reticulation process.

Copper

Copper is generally a pure metal. It conducts heat and electricity very well. Copper can be easily annealed, formed, and soldered. It is combined with many other metals to create a variety of alloys. Copper alloy 110 is a common alloy used by jewelers.

Brass

Brass is an alloy of 60 to 80% copper and 20 to 40% zinc. Alpha brass types are good for cold working, have a deep rich gold color, and usually contain less than 35% zinc. Beta brass types are good for hot working, have a pale gold color, and usually contain more than 45% zinc. Yellow brass alloy 260 and jeweler's bronze 226 are two common alloys available to jewelers.

Pewter

Pewter is an alloy of 85 to 99% tin, with the remainder antimony and copper. It has a very low melting temperature of 563° Fahrenheit (295° C). It can be used in many of the same ways that other metals are used; however, you should keep a separate area and tools for working with pewter as it will contaminate and cause pits in silver and gold.

Gold

Gold can generally be substituted for work in any of the projects described in this book. When using hot metal techniques, purchase gold solder in proper karat to match the gold chosen. Pure gold is 24 karat; standard alloys are available in 22 karat, 18 karat, 14 karat and 10 karat.

Jewelry Design

Layout

Design drawings for jewelry, due to jewelry's small scale, need to be precise. That means making detailed drawings and planning the project before getting started.

Scale drawings are a good start for your jewelry designs. Use a mechanical pencil or ink and draw out designs on paper. Use a metal ruler for straight lines if they are intended to be straight. Think about connections and how pieces will join together. Will you solder, link, or use tabs to hold your work together? Work out issues before getting started.

Time

It is important to give yourself enough time to work out the design and engineering of a piece of jewelry. Rushing through any part of the creative process usually leads to complications down the road. Take time and enjoy the creative process one step at a time. One comment frequently heard from students is that they are often impressed at the amount of time that jewelry making takes. Learning new skills and creating work gives students an understanding for the process and a new appreciation for why jewelry objects cost as much as they do.

Photo 1

Photo 2

Models

To plan and layout your jewelry, paper or thin metal can be used to make models. Cut out pieces of paper or thin metal with scissors or a sharp craft knife to create layers or to illustrate different types of metal. One of my favorite materials for making paper models is oak tag paper which is made from the same material as a manila file folder. Any type of cardstock is a good substitute. This heavier material is better because you can trace around it more easily and it will hold up longer, allowing you to reuse the patterns. It is easy to cut and can be shaped or bent to give it form in much the same way that metal can.

Transferring Patterns

Once your design is complete and you have created a paper pattern, it's time to transfer designs and lines to the metal. There are several methods. The one you choose will depend on what you are creating.

Method 1: You can choose to use an ultra-fine point permanent marker to trace around the paper pattern onto your metal.

Method 2: Scribing lines in the metal with a sharp pointed scribe is even more precise. This is the method that is preferred by many jewelers. You can draw your design freehand onto the metal with the scribe. Or, you can place a paper pattern down onto the metal and trace around it with the scribe (see photo 1).

Method 3: Consider using a glue stick to paste the paper design onto the metal and saw around the pattern or through both paper and metal at the same time (see photo 2). This method can work very well for detailed drawings on paper that won't transfer well to the metal.

Measuring

Over time, I have learned that the practicality of the metric system and the use of millimeters and centimeters wins out over using inches and fractions. A brief glance through most jewelry supply catalogs will illustrate that materials, gemstones, and findings are measured in millimeters.

Gauges

Sheet metal and stock is generally supplied in either millimeters or gauge. The B&S (Brown and Sharpe) gauge or AWS (American Wire Gauge) will be helpful to identify metal and is available from most jewelry suppliers. Gauge describes the thickness of the metal, usually in even numbers from 0 to 36. Zero is the heaviest gauge, while a higher number means thinner metal.

Ring Sizers

A set of ring sizers is another helpful tool for making a ring that fits as it should. These are available in both narrow and wide sets and help to eliminate guess work when making rings of a predetermined size.

Ring Sizers

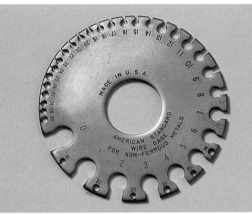

American Standard Wire Gauge

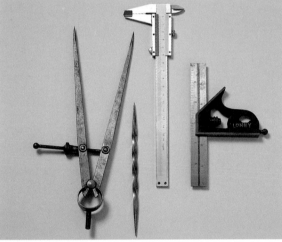

Pictured left to right: drafting divider, scribe, caliper, machinist's square

Drafting Divider

Dividers are used to measure the distance between items or for measuring equal distances between items. Find these where drawing, drafting, or jewelry making tools are found.

Scribe

A scribe is an instrument with a carbide steel tip that is used for marking the metal. I use it to transfer lines or draw my design on the metal before I begin cutting.

Calipers

This tool is used to make precise measurements. It is equipped with markings for very small measurements such as the size of stones or the thickness of sheet metal. The markings are usually offered in metric measurements.

Machinist's Square and Rulers

A steel ruler is an essential for your work bench. A square is also needed for checking the squareness or measurements of the cuts.

Cutting Lengths in MM for Metal

Ring Size	Metal Thickness			
	12 ga.	16 ga.	18 ga.	22 ga.
5	55.91	53.39	52.45	51.19
6	58.47	55.95	55.01	53.75
7	61.02	58.50	57.56	56.30
8	63.57	61.05	60.11	58.85
9	66.13	63.61	62.67	61.41
10	68.68	66.16	65.22	63.96

Safety Precautions

No one can predict the variables that might come together to create an accident. Even when practicing safety measures, sooner or later you may have an accident. Some things are inevitable when working with tools. You can expect a few cuts and scrapes here and there, and saw blades break, causing those sharp little pieces of metal to cut our skin all too easily. Learning the rules, so those accidents are minor ones rather than major ones, should be the goal. Always be aware of safe ways of working with each and every tool you use. Consider that the most dangerous areas of working are often those that are not seen. Fumes, dust, and chemicals can do far more damage to your body than tools. Seek advice from books, fellow artists, and anyone who knows more about this subject than you do. Don't wait until there is an accident to assess safety practices. Following are some important practices I would like to point out to you.

Eye Protection

Safety glasses should be one of the first tools purchased. They are the first thing that you should put on when beginning to work. A good clear pair of safety glasses is not a hindrance. Make it a priority to keep your safety glasses in tip-top shape and free of scratches so that you won't even notice wearing them.

Ear Protection

The same protection for eyes applies to ears as well. Always wear ear protection. Repeated pounding with hammers on metal produces a loud ringing noise that is damaging to the eardrum. Purchase a quality pair of earmuffs and check the decibel rating. Get in the habit of keeping them near an area where hammering and other noisy work is performed.

Tools

Using tools safely boils down to my assessment of the worst thing that this tool could do to me. If it's sharp it can cut; if it is heavy it can crush; if it has a motor then anything like clothing, hair, etc. can get wrapped around it until the motor stops.

Dust/Particulate Matter

When you are sanding, polishing, or using the flex shaft, you will create dust and particulate matter. Wipe the bench and other working surfaces down often and sweep the floors weekly. Try to keep very messy substances contained. Wearing a dust mask is helpful but it must be properly sized to the particulate. Much of the dust generated when polishing is less than one micron in size, and most dust masks will not filter out such tiny particles. Whenever possible, attempt to collect dust in a vacuum-assisted particulate collector, especially when buffing and polishing.

Chemical

Only use chemicals when absolutely necessary. If there is another less toxic option available, choose that first. Make every attempt to use chemicals out of doors with plenty of fresh air available. Another option would be to install a hood to vent the fumes outdoors. Chemical respirators are available but they must be appropriate for the type of chemical being used. Read and learn about protecting yourself before using chemicals.

Fire

Purchase quality fire extinguishers and smoke detectors. Inspect both twice a year to make sure they are in working order and that batteries are charged. Make very certain that the extinguisher will be appropriate for the type of work to be performed. Keep nothing combustible on the solder bench. Pay attention to smells, and if you smell something burning, stop and find out what it is before continuing.

CHAPTER 2

Tools & Supplies

Know your tools and what they can do. This is
the first step in learning the craft of metalsmithing.
More often than not, in this world you get what
you pay for. A cheap tool may look like a bargain,
but a substandard tool will only frustrate you in
your efforts. Conversely, it is not necessary to
purchase the most expensive tool available either.
Find a balance between cost and quality and
always purchase the highest quality tool that
you can afford.

Cutting Tools

Jeweler's Saw

A jeweler's saw is the standard tool for cutting out small detailed pieces of metal. You will need a saw frame and a variety of blade sizes. The frame is adjustable so that any blade size can be used. The size of blade needed depends upon the thickness of metal to be cut and the width of the cut desired. Matching the size of the saw blade to your metal will make sawing easier and more efficient. Generally two to three teeth of the saw blade should match the thickness of your metal. Too many teeth for a thick piece of metal means very slow sawing; too few teeth on a thin piece of metal will create a lot of chatter and a difficult to control saw frame. Your supplier will be able to help you purchase the proper size blade for your work.

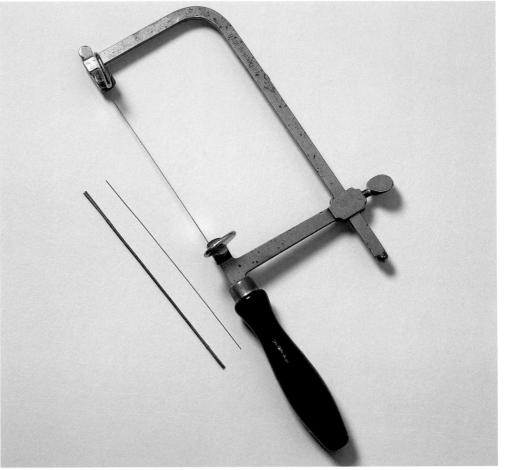

Jeweler's saw frame and blades

Bench Pin

Sawing is performed against a bench pin, which is merely a block of wood that is attached to the jeweler's bench. The bench pin can be attached to your work surface permanently by screwing it into place or temporarily with a c-clamp. It is often useful to begin sawing into the wood bench pin very lightly. This allows the blade to be guided by the wood. Then slowly and gently introduce the metal to the saw blade.

Bench pin

Saw Blade Use Chart

Metal Gauge	Size Blade
24	6/0
22	4/0 or 3/0
20-22	2/0
18-20	1/0 or 1
16-18	2-4
16	5
14	6
12	7 or 8

How to Use a Saw Blade

1. Hold the frame with the handle facing your body while seated at your table. Lean forward and use your chest to hold the saw frame between the table and your body. Your hands are free to select a saw blade. Position blade so that the teeth are facing outward.

2. Loosen one of the two setscrews and insert the blade in one. Tighten by hand (see photo 1).

3. Examine the amount of saw blade that extends towards the other setscrew. Allow a little space. The blade should not extend all the way to the other end. However, it should be close enough to be inserted into the frame when the frame is compressed.

4. Compress the frame using your chest against the table, one to two millimeters is plenty. Insert the end of the blade and tighten the setscrew (see photo 2). Test to see if the blade is under proper tension. When plucked with a fingernail it should emit a high-pitched sound rather than a dull noise.

5. Place the sheet metal on the bench pin and hold securely. The area to be cut should be over the open grooved area of the pin. Keep the saw blade as vertical as possible. Use the entire length of the blade to make the cut, moving in a long and precise movement (see photo 3). Don't seesaw the blade. Turn the metal as you cut, don't turn the saw.

Photo 1

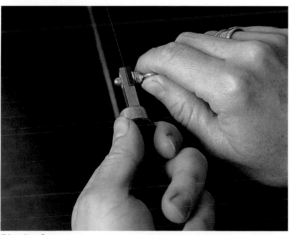

Photo 2

Photo 3

Practice, practice, practice

Sawing is a fundamental skill that you will use over and over, so it is important to master it. Get used to breaking a lot of blades. Sawing is one of the aspects of jewelry making that people will either embrace or become frustrated with. Try to embrace it and see how far you can saw before you break a blade. If you are not breaking blades you are not doing much sawing.

A teacher of mine once said, "Pretend the handle of the saw frame is a baby bird." Grasp it firmly enough to hold the saw frame in position, but avoid the "white knuckle" technique. Above all, try to relax and enjoy this process. Pay attention to your hand, the metal, and the repetition of the saw going up and down. Find the balance and strive for perfection in every action you perform, each time you do it.

Cutting Tools

Jewelry Pliers

Jewelry pliers are necessary for holding and forming work. Note that you need jewelry pliers, not regular handyman pliers. You will find these where jewelry supplies are sold. Flat pliers are good for general holding. Round-nose pliers are useful for creating round or curved pieces, especially with wire. Chain-nose pliers are used for working with small jump rings and chain making. Parallel pliers are useful for holding work that is of a square cross section and for straightening bent wire. Half-round pliers are a necessity when making rings and other round forms.

Snips and Shears

Snips are useful for cutting wire. Wire cutters can also be used for cutting wire. Many pliers have a snipping section. You should have several types of snips to use, small ones for snipping fine wire and larger ones for heavier wire.

Hand shears are sometimes useful. They do not provide a clean, precise cut as the jeweler's saw does, but are great for rough cutting of large pieces of metal quickly. Hand shears tear the metal and do not leave a nice flush edge as sawing does. Shearing also deforms the metal and care must be used to prevent unnecessary warping.

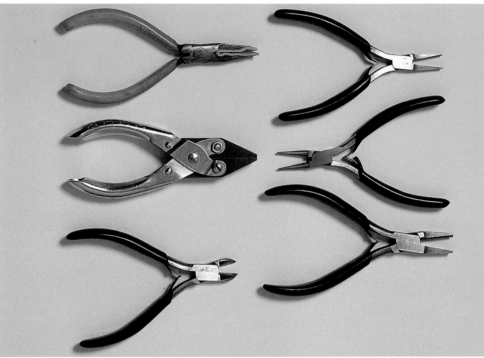

Clockwise from top: Pliers lined with leather to protect work, flat-nose pliers, round-nose pliers, chain-nose pliers, wire cutters, parallel pliers

Snips

Disk Cutter

These tools are also called circle punches. They are used to cut pieces of sheet metal into perfect circles. Metal is inserted into the slot between the two blocks and a corresponding size punch is inserted into the chosen sized hole. A hammer strike on the punch shears the metal. A hydraulic press can also be used to press the punch.

Disk Cutter

Finishing Tools

Files

Once the metal is cut, it is necessary to file the edges smooth. This is done with a series of files that remove small bits of metal. Files come in a variety of sizes, a variety of shapes, and in varying tooth surfaces. Files are generally used to create straight edges, but can also be used creatively for making decorative edges on metal.

For the majority of work, the most useful shape is the half round file. The half round file can be used for flat edges, rounded convex, and concave shapes. All the file lengths, including the smaller needle files, are available in a range of shapes and cuts. The file surface or tooth cuts range from coarse to fine. A rough, medium, and fine cut are a good choice for doing a range of work.

Files cut on the pushing stroke. Begin with the coarsest file needed depending on how much metal needs to be removed. With the work held firmly in a ring clamp and that held firmly against a bench pin, hold the file with the tip end against the

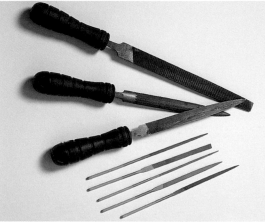
A variety of files to have on hand

Emery paper and sanding sticks

Using a file to smooth edge

metal and push firmly and evenly across the metal. As you file, take a very close look at the work to make certain that the file is removing the metal needed and not taking too much away. Use pressure to gently and evenly guide the file across your work. Lift the file after each stroke. Don't get lazy and let the file drag back and forth across the surface. Also, take your time working the edges using files from coarse to fine until you achieve a very smooth edge.

Emery Paper

To remove even smaller amounts of metal and further refine the shape, switch from the file to emery paper. It is like sandpaper except it utilizes an abrasive called silicon carbide that is suited for use on metal. Emery paper is available

in a range of grits from 100 to 600. The number refers to the number of pieces of grit per square inch. In general, use 220, 320, 400, and 600 in that order when working towards a high polish. Sanding is performed in advance of soldering to clean up surfaces and after soldering when working towards a finished surface. Other types of finishing papers in finer grits (ranging in microns) are very useful for very fine polishing.

Sanding sticks can be purchased, or you can make your own by wrapping emery paper around a flat wooden piece such as a wooden ruler. Use a flat sanding stick on a flat surface so you won't make grooves or create an irregular surface.

Burnishing Tool

This tool is highly polished and used for polishing edges of metal. It is also used to aid in setting stones into bezels.

TIPS

- Every time a file rubs against the metal small pieces are being removed. It is possible to file or sand your metal away.

- When you are filing or sanding, remove sharp burs as they occur.

- Strive to keep surfaces free of scratches as you work.

Drilling Tools & Accessories

Drills

Drills are available in a variety of materials and sizes. For metal, make certain that drill bits are high-speed steel (HSS) or titanium nitride (TiN) coated. For general work, drill bits should be sharpened to a 118° angle. For heavier metals such as steel, they should be sharpened to a 150° angle. Drill bits are available in sets of fractional inches and numbered sizes from 0 to 80. Very small drills bits from 60-80 are so small that they need to be held in a drill with very small jaws or a flexible shaft tool. When drilling very large holes, make a smaller hole first and incrementally work up to the finished hole size. Step bits are also available for drilling large holes in thin metal.

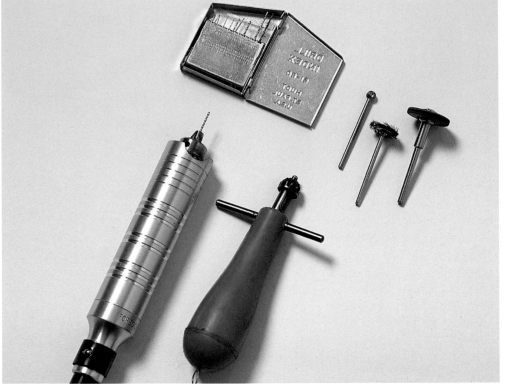

Pictured clockwise from top: drill bits, flex shaft tools, chuck key, flex shaft hand piece

Flexible Shaft Machine

The flexible shaft machine is an indispensable tool for the jeweler. It consists of a small motor that is generally suspended from a hook. Below the motor is a flexible shaft attached to a hand piece. A foot control is a convenient device to control the speed of the flex shaft when one hand is holding the drill and the other hand is holding the work. Many different hand pieces are available for specialized purposes, but for general work a standard hand piece is sufficient. The hand piece works in much the same way a drill chuck does.

A small chuck key is used to tighten and loosen a three-jaw chuck that holds drills and other tools. The flex shaft can serve the role of a drill for small drill bits. Other rotary tools such as burrs, sanding tools, and a host of other devices are used in the flex shaft.

To insert a drill bit or any other rotary device, use the chuck key to open the three-jaw chuck on the hand piece. Remember, righty tighty, lefty loosey! Insert the tool until it is seated in the chuck. Tighten the chuck with the chuck key and take care to keep the drill centered between the three jaws, and not in between two of the three jaws. A quick rotation of the chuck will cause the drill to spin in a circle if it is not centered.

TIPS
- Small drill bits are very fragile and tend to break easily. Feed the drill bit slowly into the metal and allow it to cut. Do not force or bend the drill. Try to avoid breaking drill bits and keep extras on hand.

- For best results, lubricate the drill bit with beeswax before you begin drilling.

Center Punch

A center punch is a sharp tool for making an indentation in metal. While drilling a hole, a drill bit will often "walk" across the metal and the hole will not end up precisely where you intended. Before drilling, use a center punch and a hammer to create a very small dimple in the metal to help keep the drill centered. Use a steel block under the metal or the punch will create a much larger depression in the metal. Also, when creating a large circle with a pair of dividers, use the center punch to mark the center of the circle.

Steel Block

Use a steel block that is a minimum of 4 inches (10.2 cm) square x 1 inch (2.5 cm) thick. This will provide a level, sturdy work surface for hammering, punching, or stamping designs into metal. One surface is ground and sanded flat to avoid unnecessary marks made in the reverse side of metal while it is being worked. An anvil is a great tool for stamping, hammering, and forming metal, but a steel bench block is a suitable substitute for small work.

Center punch shown with a steel block and a hammer

Making an indentation on a pendant piece using a center punch

CAUTIONS

- Drilling creates friction and that means heat! Take care when drilling to protect your hand and fingers from the metal that gets hot while drilling.

- It is wise to hold the metal in a drill vise or use something such as a block of wood that will anchor it if it gets caught on the drill and spins around.

- Never attempt to stop a piece of metal spinning on a drill bit with your hand; it will cut like a knife.

- Take care to protect your work surface from drill bits that pierce the metal and anything below it. Use blocks of wood beneath the metal. This will also help to reduce the size of the bur created around the underside of the hole.

Holding Tools

Vise

This tool is indispensable to holding objects tightly while working on them. It is best to permanently attach it to a wooden bench or sturdy work surface using screws. This will keep it from moving while working on your metal. The metal is placed into the jaws of the vise and the handle is used to tighten the jaws on the metal. Use leather to protect the surface of the metal pieces while in the vise if necessary.

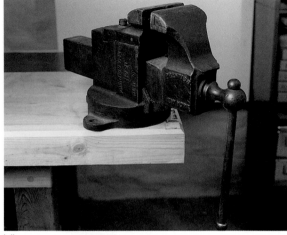
Vise

Ring Clamp

This handy tool is not used exclusively for holding rings. It is designed to hold small pieces of work and reduce fatigue on the hand. Small pieces of metal to be filed can be inserted into the clamp, which has one flat and one curved end. Metal is inserted into one end and a wedge inserted into the opposite end. This will contain whatever small object needs to be held, usually for filing or polishing. The ring clamp can be held against the bench pin at whatever angle needed to perform a multitude of tasks.

Ring Clamp

Filing Block

A filing block is a handy tool for filing metal edges at a precise angle. The hardened steel block cannot be filed, but allows the user to file down to the surface of the block. Precision ground angles of 45° and 90° are useful for creating frames and miters when creating square corners.

Tweezers

Tweezers are handy helpers and have a multitude of uses. When things are too small for your fingers to pick up, tweezers are needed. One or two pair of tweezers are needed for soldering. A pair of copper or wooden tongs is needed for holding jewelry while going in and out of the pickle pot during the soldering process.

Pictured top to bottom: larger tweezers, small tweezers, copper tongs.

Filing Block

Mandrels

Ring and bracelet mandrels are two useful tools that are used when forming jewelry. These heavy metal mandrels are best held in a vise while they are being used. The metal is formed around these tools by striking the metal with a mallet against the mandrel form. Sizes are marked on the mandrels so that you can form the piece to the size needed.

Mandrels

Here's How

Slide the metal jewelry piece onto the mandrel in the position needed to create the desired size. Strike the metal piece with a mallet to create the rounded shape of a ring or a bracelet.

Stakes

Stakes are made of metal, wood, or nylon. A stake is held in a vise while the metal is hammered into shape. Many different stakes are available for a variety of shapes and types. Hitting the metal against the stake is a method of stretching the metal.

Creative metalsmiths will make their own stakes and forming tools when specific needs arise. Often an old wooden stump will be improvised with different shaped depressions carved into it. Metal can be hammered into these forms with hammers and tools in order to give it shape and form. More highly specialized metal forms called dies are created when a long lasting shape is required.

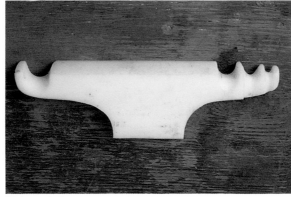
Nylon stake

Here's How

Secure the stake in a vise. Place the jewelry piece into the stake shape of your choice. Strike piece with a hammer to form. Shown here, a bracelet is taking on a concave form.

25

Forming Tools

Hammers

Jewelers tend to own a lot of hammers. Different shapes and sizes are useful for different tasks.

- A general hammer that weighs about one to two pounds is needed for hitting tools such as the disc cutter, center punch, and other decorative punches.
- A chasing hammer is used with chasing tools that form and impart textures on the metal surface.
- Silversmithing hammers are used to strike the metal, forming or stretching it as needed. They are very specialized hammers that are polished to a mirror like finish. They are never used to hit another tool which would damage the hammer's pristine surface.
- Planishing hammers are also highly polished and are used to impart different hammered textures to the metal. The metal is hammered against a steel block or a shaping stake and the hammer is used to strike the surface of the metal.
- Round-faced, ball peen, and cross peen hammers are used to stretch, texture, and form metal.
- A caulking hammer is used to upset edges or make them heavier by hammering them on edge against a steel block.

A hammer will deform or stretch the metal in different ways depending on the size, shape, the material it is made from, and the amount of force used by the person wielding it. The surface

Pictured from left: planishing hammer, ball peen/round faced, cross peen, caulking, textured hammer

behind the metal being struck also influences the way in which the metal moves, bends and deforms. Metal can be struck against air, a sand-bag, wood, plastic, or steel; each of these will produce a different result. In general, a harder hammer, tool, or work surface will produce greater deformation and stronger marks in the metal. It will also cause the metal to become harder more quickly; this is called *work hardening*. The opposite is true of softer hammers and tools made of wood, plastic, and rawhide.

A round-faced hammer will stretch metal in all directions. A cross peen hammer will stretch metal in two directions. Understanding the tool's application and how metal moves and behaves is learned only through trial and error. Experiment with scrap metal and hammer it in various ways to appreciate the many ways it can be shaped and textured with various tools and hammers. Keep these samples, as they are often a source of inspiration when designing and creating new work.

Using a cross peen hammer to texture metal

Using a round-faced hammer to flatten and stretch the metal

Mallets

A rawhide, wooden, or plastic mallet can be used to flatten or form sheet metal without leaving too many hammer marks. The metal is usually formed over a stake or mandrel.

Pictured from left: rawhide mallet, plastic mallet

Here's How

Place the metal piece on a work surface such as a steel block, a mandrel, or a stake. Strike to form the malleable metal. Shown here, a rawhide mallet is being used to form the metal strip around a ring mandrel.

Chasing Tools

Chasing tools are punches or stamps that have a design on one end. They are made of hard steel and are rod-shaped like pencils. They impart a design or texture to the metal. A light chasing hammer is used to strike the non-design end of the tool while the design end is against the metal. A wide variety of designs are available from jeweler suppliers.

This shows the ends of the chasing tools, revealing the designs that can be stamped into the metal

Here's How

When stamping a design into the metal with a chasing tool, always place the metal on a steel block work surface. Strike only once or the tool will cause a shadow impression. Striking once with the correct force will give a sharp impression. This will take some practice.

Forming Tools

Dapping Block & Tools

This square metal block, called a dapping block, has various sized round depressions and corresponding dapping punches. Small pieces of metal can be formed into shallow or deep half-round forms. Generally, metal disks and round forms are used in the dapping block, though any shape can be formed as long as it fits within the cavity. After placing the metal into the block form, insert the dapping tool in the dapping block and make certain that it fits down into the form. Begin in a hollow form that is larger than the metal. Work slowly to smaller and smaller depressions with corresponding smaller dapping tools until the desired shape is achieved. For items that have textured surfaces, place a small circle of leather in the bottom of the hole to protect the surface of the metal against the dapping block.

Once the dapping is complete, sand the outside edge flat on emery paper. This flat edge can be soldered to another piece of metal or polished to create a finished edge. If you intend to solder two dapped pieces together, file a small hole along one edge of the pieces or drill a hole in one piece to allow for expansion of gasses when soldering any enclosed hollow form.

Here's How

A brass metal disk is placed into the bottom of one form on the block. The dapping punch is placed into the form and struck with a hammer to form the metal.

Rolling Mill

A rolling mill is used to compress metal and create thinner pieces of sheet or wire. It can also be used to impart textures and surface embellishment on metal in a technique called roller printing. The rolling mill is a heavy and expensive piece of equipment. It is not a tool you will need if you are just beginning. Only if you plan to do a lot of this type of fabrication would you need this type of tool.

A hand crank powers two steel rolls through which the metal is compressed. The rolls can be adjusted up and down to allow for different thickness of metal and materials to be printed.

The topmost crank, which adjusts the distance between the rolls, should only be turned from one quarter to a half of a turn to slowly reduce metal in thickness. Any greater reduction will be too difficult to crank. Test the gap between the rolls with two pieces of scrap metal that are the same gauge as the material to be used. The metal should be a tight fit between the rolls.

When roller printing, a variety of materials can be used to give texture. Paper, sandpaper, dried leaves, plant materials, fabric, metal screening, and perforated metal are all materials that give surprising effects in metal.

Testing different materials with varying amounts of pressure and varied metals will give you an idea of what is possible.

Always sandwich the material to be roller printed between two pieces of metal in order to protect the rolls themselves. The rolls will lengthen and stretch the metal, so care should be exercised when attempting to create a piece of a specific size.

Here's How

Place the material to be imprinted onto the metal piece. Insert this between the adjusted rollers and crank. Here a dried fern leaf is being used to make a fern impression.

Hydraulic Press

The hydraulic press is another expensive piece of equipment that is not required, but is convenient for jewelers doing a lot of die work. Presses are available in a range of sizes and with hydraulic jacks of varying pressures. The hydraulic jack is contained within the press frame. As the piston is extended, pressure builds within the frame and on anything that is trapped between the piston and the frame. Simple dies can be made to cut and shape metal and can be used repeatedly.

Here's How

Tape the steel wire and metal piece down to a steel block to prevent movement. Place the steel block with the metal taped to it into the hydraulic press. Place another steel block over the steel/metal sandwich. Crank the hydraulic cylinder using moderate force to press the die into the silver. Release the pressure and check impression. Remember, it is always easy to do more, but over-doing it means re-doing it.

Soldering Tools

Soldering is the art of joining two pieces of metal. Soldering is accomplished with high heat and solder material that melts and acts like a glue to hold the pieces together.

Soldering Torch

Many types and sizes of torches are available. For general jewelry use, choose a torch that uses fuel and atmospheric (what we are breathing) air. Propane, acetylene, and natural gas are the preferred gasses used by most jewelers. Choose a torch that fits your needs based on the size of work and the availability of fuel gas. For general work, a hand held torch with several different sized tips will allow for a wide range of soldering tasks.

Torches require regulators to limit the flow of gas to the torch. A separate regulator is needed for each gas. Do not mix and match regulators with different gasses. If you don't know or understand what type of regulator to use, consult a welding supplier or catalog.

Practice extreme caution when using a torch. Before attempting to solder, gain knowledge by taking a class or learning from a teacher who can guide you through the process.

Pictured clockwise from top: flux in round container, flux brush, striker, solder pick, three sizes of torch heads

Solder

Solder is an alloy that melts at a lower temperature than the jewelry metal. Solder is available in silver and gold alloys. Silver solder and gold solder are hard solders, much different from soft solder used in plumbing. Silver solder is generally used on copper, brass, and bronze; however, it does not provide a good color match for these metals.

Solder is available in sheet, wire, and paste form. Choosing one over the other is a matter of preference. The type of seam also influences the choice of solder. Many jewelers prefer flat chips of solder that can be placed precisely where needed, while others prefer wire that can be held with tweezers and introduced into the seam at the precise melting point. Another method of adding solder is to melt pieces of solder with a torch until they draw up into a ball, then pick them up with a solder pick and drop onto the fluxed seam.

Hard solders melt at high temperatures and create a bond that is almost as strong as the metal itself. Because different solders have varying melting points, you can solder successive joints on the same work without the worry of melting the previous seams. For example, *hard silver solder* melts at 1425° Fahrenheit (773.9° C). You could solder the first joint with hard solder then the next joint with *medium silver solder* that melts at 1390° Fahrenheit (754.4° C) to avoid melting the first joint. Successive joints can be soldered with *easy silver solder* which melts at 1325° Fahrenheit (718.3° C). *Extra easy silver solder* is also available and melts at 1270° Fahrenheit (187.7° C). Lastly, there is *IT solder* which flows at 1490° Fahrenheit (810° C) for extra hard solder joints.

Flux & Brush

Flux is an oxygen absorbing material used to inhibit oxides from forming on metal during the soldering process. Fluxes are generally borax compounds, but often contain poisonous substances. Do not breathe the fumes when soldering and wash hands after touching flux. Apply flux sparingly with a small brush in a thin layer. Flux only the area where you are soldering because the solder will flow only on the fluxed areas. Avoid painting flux on to the entire work.

Binding Wire

Binding wire or steel wire is a preferred material to hold work in place while soldering. Use pliers to twist the wire securely and also to tighten the wire around the material to be soldered. Make certain to remove the binding wire from the work before placing it in the pickle solution.

Investment

Investment is a plaster-like material that can be used to hold work together while soldering. After joining the pieces to be soldered with quick drying glue, mold the investment around the work. After soldering, the investment will dissolve in water. Do not wash this down the drain.

Solder Pick

A solder pick can be as simple and low tech as a piece of old coat hanger wire or as high tech as titanium, to which solder will not stick. Whatever you prefer will work. A solder pick aids in placing and moving solder when the work is too hot to touch.

Soldering Surface

Lightweight ceramic firebrick or specialized ceramic tiles are good choices for a light, reflective surface. It is imperative that the solder table and surrounding items be fireproof.

Tweezers

A very fine pair is useful for picking up and placing small chips of solder, and a larger pair is needed for quenching work when soldering is complete. A pair of copper or wooden tongs is needed for jewelry that is going in and out of the pickle pot.

Pickle and Pickle Pot

Pickle is a mild acid solution of sodium bisulphate and water. It is used to remove flux and metal oxides after soldering. Most often it is used in a warming pot to speed up its effectiveness. Never use steel or stainless steel tweezers to fetch your work from the pickle as it will deposit copper oxide on your metal and your tweezers.

Ventilation

Soldering produces fumes that should be exhausted with a ventilated hood. Never rely on the air exchange in the room to provide adequate ventilation. Toxic fumes inhaled can accumulate in your body and cause a wide range of health problems.

CAUTIONS

- Gasses are under extreme pressure, so learn how to use your regulator.

- When setting up a torch or changing a tank of gas, always use soap bubbles to test for leaks in the fittings between the tank, regulator, hose, and torch. Any leak will cause the soap bubbles to grow large and highlight the source of the leak.

- Always secure gas tanks to the leg of a bench or a wall. A fallen tank could leak or break the regulator.

- Turn tanks off completely when not in use. Bleed the gas from the lines until no gas escapes to make certain that all traces of gas have been flushed out.

- Always have a fire extinguisher and bucket of water handy for unforeseen fires. If you smell something burning, stop and find out what it is. Never wait to see what that funny burning smell was—find it and put it out.

- The pickle solution can irritate. Wash with cold water immediately if it comes in contact with skin.

- Allow only copper tongs to come in contact with the pickle solution.

- Don't plunge hot metal into pickle solution. Either quench the metal in water first or allow metal to air cool.

Polishing Tools & Supplies

Buffing & Polishing Machine

Polishing is the final step in finishing. Buffing and polishing remove very small amounts of metal to turn a rough surface into a smooth one. A high polish is a lot of work to achieve and to maintain as it will show all scratches and marks from normal wear and tear.

To create this wonderful light-reflective finish, you will need a buffing machine or polishing machine that has a $1/4$ to $1/2$ hp motor and tapered spindles to attach various polishing buffs. It should always be used in conjunction with a dust collection system as polishing compounds contain small particles of silica which should not be inhaled.

Work should be held preferably in your gloved hand, or very small parts can be held with a ring clamp. Buffing creates a lot of friction and metal can heat up to be too hot to hold in a matter of seconds. A bowl of water nearby is useful to cool work while buffing.

Buffing & polishing machine

Polishing buffs, wheels, and polishing compounds

Pictured clockwise from top: drill bits, flex shaft tools, chuck key, flex shaft hand piece

Polishing Buffs/Wheels

These are wheels made of felt, leather or muslin with a hole in the center where they are attached to a tapered spindle on the buffing machine. Buffs are available stitched or unstitched, with the stitched buffs providing a denser surface for polishing. A general size polishing buff for most work is 6 inches (15.2 cm) in diameter. Smaller buffs are also available and useful for getting into small areas.

Flexible Shaft Machine

Polishing very small items is possible with the flexible shaft and tiny polishing tools. Be careful to use on only very small items as small polishing tools on large work tends to create small ridges and lines.

Buffing/Polishing Compounds

Have on hand a range of abrasive compounds to be used in succession in much the same way as using emery paper. Compounds come in bars and are applied to a spinning buff. Two or maybe three compounds are generally enough for most polishing procedures. Choose a compound that is right for the type of metal you are using.

Dedicate a buff for each compound and never interchange compounds on buffs. Clean your work thoroughly between compounds to prevent contamination from one compound to another. If "skid marks" or lines of compound begin to deposit on your work, stop to remove them with a solution of warm water, a few drops of dish soap, and a splash of ammonia. This all-purpose cleaner is great for removing buffing compound from your work and your hands. Use a very soft brush or cloth when using cleaner.

Brass Brush

A brash brush is a handy tool for removing oxidized areas left after pickling. It can also be used to create a *scratch-brush finish*. This is a random pattern created by rubbing the brass bristles across metal in a circular motion. It creates a slightly satin finish.

Brass brush

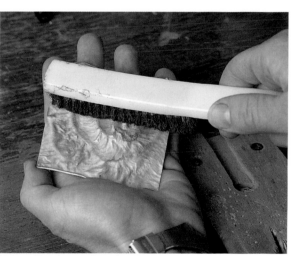
Using the brass brush

CAUTION
The polishing machine is one of the most dangerous tools in the shop and should be approached with caution. The motor spins at 3450 revolutions per minute and can grab anything close to it—your work, loose clothing, and your hair. It can grab these things in a fraction of a second and send them back to you mangled, broken, or stripped away.

CHAPTER 3

Techniques

In this chapter, you will use what you learned about your tools to put those tools to work. Even though there are many techniques presented in this chapter, you won't need to master all of them to begin making jewelry. Once you learn how to saw, pierce, drill, and forge, you will be surprised at the many pieces of jewelry you can make.

Piercing

Piercing refers to sawing out an interior shape in the metal. For this pictured example, a spiral design was pierced into the metal.

You will need
- Metal of choice
- Jeweler's saw and blade
- Beeswax or saw blade lubricant
- Scribe
- Center punch
- Hammer
- Steel block
- Drill with fine drill bit
- Bench pin or board for drilling surface

Step 1
Use a scribe to draw the design on your metal. Here, we are using a scribe to make a mark for a center hole where the spiral design will begin. The scribe makes a faint scratch mark in the metal. This can be polished out later if the marks show after sawing.

Step 2
Use the center punch and a hammer to mark the hole in the center of the metal piece. Work on a steel block and use a hammer to strike the center punch once. This mark will help to keep the drill centered.

TIP
A center punch dents the metal so that the drill won't "walk" across it. The bit will be more likely to follow the indention that has been marked. Work on a steel block and use a hammer to strike the center punch one time.

Step 3

Using a small drill bit, drill a hole into the center of disk where it has been indented with the center punch. Use the bench pin or a wood block as a surface for your drilling.

TIP

For best results, lubricate the drill bit with beeswax before you begin drilling.

Step 4

Insert a saw blade into one end of the saw frame. Thread the other end of the saw blade through the hole in the metal. Move the metal to be cut towards the end of the saw where the blade is fixed. Fasten the saw blade in the frame with the metal piece in place.

Step 5

Place the metal piece on the bench pin. Begin piercing at the center hole, moving the saw blade up and down vertically while keeping the blade perfectly perpendicular to the metal. Slowly move the metal around in a spiral while sawing up and down.

TIP

Do not change the position of the saw blade quickly or it will simply bend and perhaps break. Be sure to move the saw up and down in the sawing motion as you are slowly changing the position of the metal.

Stamping

Stamping is the process of imparting a design into the metal using chasing or stamping tools. The process is very simple, yet the results can be awesome. The design end of the stamping tool is placed on the metal while a hammer strikes the other end of the tool. Use a metal block as your work surface, placing it on a wooden surface such as the floor or a sturdy work bench to absorb the blows of the hammer. Experiment on scrap metal until you achieve the desired result. Try using lighter and heavier hammers for more subtle or dramatic results.

You will need

- Metal of choice
- Chasing or stamping tools
- Hammer
- Steel block

TIPS

- For stamping, choose metal sheet or wire that is a minimum of 18-gauge thick. Using metal any thinner than this will not give a good impression when stamped.

- Always wear ear and eye protection while working. Keep your fingers out of the way of the hammer and stamp.

Stamping a design into ring

Step 1

Hold the stamp using thumb and forefinger. Anchor your hand and wrist on metal block and any surrounding surface. Rock the stamp back and forth slightly to make certain that it is flat on the surface of the metal. Check spacing and placement of stamps by looking at the reflection of the stamp in the metal as it is near the surface of the metal.

Step 2

Strike the stamp squarely and solidly with the hammer. Attempt to do this only once as repeated stamping while the stamp is in the same place often creates multiple impressions. Think about trying to drive the stamp down into the metal to create a good impression, not just hitting the top of the stamp. Keep the stamping strong, but not so deep so as to shear the metal. If you are going to repeat the stamped design, move and align the stamp and repeat the procedure.

TIP

For very precise alignment of designs or letters, use a piece of tape as a guide for the bottom edge of the stamp.

Forging

Forging is the process of shaping and forming the metal by striking with a hammer. Nonferrous metals such as silver, gold, and other metals can be forged without heat. *Planishing* is the final step in forging. Planishing smooths out any irregularities in the metal and gives it an overall smooth surface and evenly hammered surface. The planishing marks can be left as a decorative hammered surface or sanded and polished out, depending upon the desired surface.

You will need
- Metal of choice
- Hammer, such as a cross peen, ball peen, or planishing
- Steel block

Step 1
Strike the metal, keeping your hammer strokes even. Pay close attention so that the metal is forged out symmetrically.

Step 2
Hammer until the metal does not move.

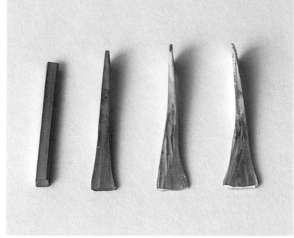

These examples show how a square metal wire was shaped using a cross peen hammer. A fan-shaped effect was desired so a cross peen hammer was used to stretch the metal in two directions.

TIPS
- Hammers and steel block working surfaces must be kept polished so they will not impart unwanted marks to the metal jewelry pieces.

- The shape of the hammer you choose is very important. Each type of hammer moves the metal in a specific way. A cross peen hammer will move the metal in two directions. A ball peen will push the metal outward in all directions. Practice with your hammers to see how they move and shape the metal.

Annealing

Metal needs to be malleable (or soft) in order to be bent, shaped, or hammered so that it will not to break. Annealing is used to soften the metal, relieve internal stresses, refine the structure, and improve cold working properties. Most metals are sold half-hard and ready to work. However, during the working process, the metal may become hardened before you finish the design. In order to make it softer and workable again, you may need to anneal the metal piece. In general, the annealing process is the act of heating the metal and then quickly quenching it in water.

Malleability

This is the property of metal that allows it to be bent, formed, stamped, or shaped without breaking. Metal has a range of softness to hardness that varies for each type. Most metals for jewelry making are sold in a half-hard state. However, many suppliers will supply metal in a fully annealed or dead-soft state when asked. You can begin fabricating your metal as purchased, but too much forming without annealing may begin to make the metal brittle. Depending on the range of tasks to be performed, sooner or later your metal will need to be annealed before you go any further.

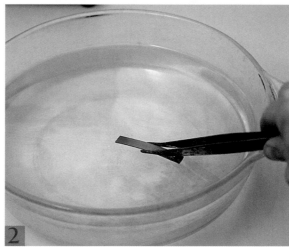

Heating Times

Annealing times differ for each metal. For silver and gold and most non-ferrous and precious metals, heat the work on a clean firebrick to approximately 1100° Fahrenheit (593.3° C). This is also the temperature when white paste flux turns clear, so using a small dab of flux will give a good indication of temperature. Heat copper until a dull red glow is seen in the metal. Brass should actually glow red before quenching. Air-cooling after heating most metals will increase or maintain the previous level of hardness.

You will need
- Metal of choice
- Torch
- Container of water
- Pickle & pickle pot
- Firebrick
- Tweezers

Step 1

Place the metal piece on a firebrick. Light the torch and adjust so that you have a large brushy flame. Heat the entire piece of metal, moving the torch continuously over the metal piece. Keep the torch moving at all times. The metal will change to a faint reddish hue when it approaches the annealing temperature. Annealing is best performed in a darkened area so that the true color of the metal can be seen.

Step 2

Allow the metal to fade to black then quickly extinguish the torch. Grab the metal with tweezers and quench it in water. Next, dip the metal in the pickle solution.

Preventing and Removing Fire Scale

Heating any metal during annealing or soldering will produce a layer of metal oxide on the surface of the metal referred to as *fire scale*. For most metals, this can be stripped away in the pickle solution. Care must be exercised to prevent overheating of the metal, especially when working with sterling silver, brass, and low karat gold. These metals, when overheated, will have a layer of copper oxide bonded to the top layer of metal. It appears as a pinkish glow and is often indiscernible to the untrained eye. When polishing, fire scale often appears adjacent to an area that has been sanded and polished. It is difficult to remove fire scale once it appears, so keep annealing and heating to a minimum.

Several techniques for working to avoid fire scale are available. The first is to attempt to heat as little as possible and not to overheat when soldering and annealing. The second is to work with a new sterling alloy called argentium sterling. This is a standard alloy and is still 92.5% silver, but replaces some of the copper in standard sterling silver (which produces the fire scale) with germanium, which does not produce fire scale.

Remove fire scale by dipping metal into a pickle solution.

When to Anneal

Once annealed, the metal will maintain its malleability until worked on again. While working on your piece, it can be annealed as many times as necessary to keep it from becoming brittle or cracking. Use heating and quenching judiciously to maintain the integrity of the metal, especially in the last steps of assembling a piece of jewelry.

See page 100 for stamped ring instructions.

Oxidizing

Most metals, such as silver, copper, brass, or unsealed iron will oxidize naturally. Oxidation is a chemical reaction of the metal bonding with oxygen to form a discoloration (and in some cases a corrosion) on the metal surface. Oxidation can create depth and definition to jewelry designs that have texture or designs stamped onto the surface. But you don't have to wait for nature; you can speed up the process by oxidizing the metal yourself. The term *patina* is often used to describe the result of this process.

You will need

- Metal alloy containing copper, or pure copper
- Liver of sulfur
- Mixing bowl
- Water
- Brush
- Polishing compound and buffing machine
- Jewelry polishing cloth

Liver of sulfur

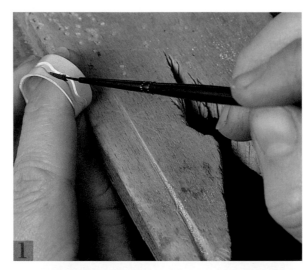

Oxidizing Solutions

Many chemicals will turn copper and metals containing copper black, or a range of colors from gray to blue to brown. Liver of sulfur is one of the chemicals that is used most often to oxidize jewelry metal. As its name implies, it smells strongly of sulfur. You can mix your own solution or purchase it ready mixed. Other chemicals are available to create a wide range of colors and effects; however, most of these use very toxic chemicals.

CAUTION

Always use liver of sulfur in a well-ventilated area. Fumes should not be inhaled. Use gloves, respirators, and eye protection. Work out of doors whenever possible.

Step 1

Place a pea-sized lump of liver of sulfur in a bowl of water to make an oxidizing solution. Paint the solution onto the metal with a brush to blacken copper, brass or sterling silver. Alternately, you can drop the jewelry piece in the solution. Remove piece from the solution when it has turned gray or black. Allow to dry.

Step 2

Polish the piece with polishing compound on the buffing machine to remove unwanted oxidation. Finish with a polishing cloth to create a shine. The oxidation will usually remain in the crevices. If it hasn't remained in the crevices, use a fine paint brush to *carefully* paint it in. Use a hand polishing cloth to remove any excess.

TIPS

- Always mix a new liver of sulfur solution for each working session.
- Jewelry piece must be clean and free of grease. Wash jewelry under warm water or pickle to clean it.
- Keep unmixed liver of sulfur tightly sealed so it stays dry.

Working with Wire

Metal wire is a wonderful material for making beautiful jewelry pieces such as rings, bracelets, and linked necklaces. Findings such as ear wires, hooks, clasps, and jump rings can be easily made with wire. I always keep a variety of wire gauges on hand. Learning how to bend the wire is a basic technique.

Step 1

With wire cutters or pliers, snip wire to the size needed for the design piece. Cut a little more than you think you will need. The ends can be trimmed after you have bent the wire in the desired shape. Be sure to use wire cutters that are appropriate to the gauge of wire to be cut. Using too light a pair of cutters on heavy wire will mash the wire instead of cutting it.

Step 2

Use half round or round-nose pliers to gently bend the wire. Precious metal wire is usually sold fully annealed. If yours is not, annealing the wire before you begin with it will make it easier to bend. If your wire is springy it will not bend easily or hold its shape and should be annealed. When making a spiral or curved design, place the pliers at the end of the wire and use your fingers to bend the wire, at the same time turning the pliers.

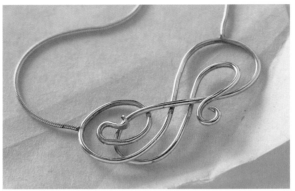

It takes only a little practice to be able to bend wire gracefully to create a design such as this pendant.

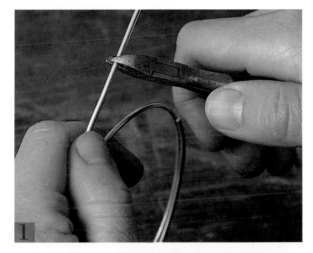

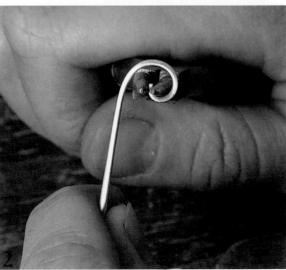

Making Jump Rings

Jump rings are round wire rings or links used to attach findings to finished work. Jump rings can be made from any size or shape of wire. Ready-made jump rings are also available.

TIPS

• If square ends on the wire are important, use a jeweler's saw to cut them or file the ends of the wire to make a smooth and refined end.

• The end of the wire can be filed to make a tapered end.

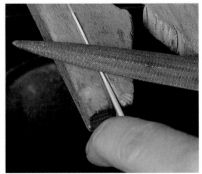

• Cover the ends of the pliers in plastic dip coating (usually used on the handles), tape, or leather to prevent them from making unwanted marks on the metal. Pliers with nylon jaws are also available but often they are not to be found in the shape needed for the desired result.

Making Links

Jump rings and links can be purchased, but they are easy to make. When you know how to make a link, it is then easy to join them to create a variety of beautiful necklace chains. Links are formed by wrapping precious metal wire around a dowel. The dowel acts as a mandrel. Choose a dowel the same diameter you want for the finished link. Be sure the dowel is long enough for wrapping the required number of links.

You will need

- Metal wire in desired gauge
- Dowel
- Drill bits and flexible shaft machine
- Bench pin
- Jeweler's saw
- Saw blades
- Flat-nosed pliers, two pairs

Step 1

Drill a tiny hole crosswise in one end of the dowel. The hole should be as large as the wire gauge you are using. Pass one end of the wire through this hole. Bend it to securely hold it in place.

Step 2

Wrap the wire around the dowel, keeping it taut with the wraps close together. Make as many wraps as needed for the number of links you desire.

Step 3

Hold the coiled wire around the dowel, pushing it against the bench pin. (Or you can remove the wood dowel if the wire is stout enough and can be held by hand.) Saw through the wire coils to make the links. To assist in guiding the saw blade while cutting, saw into the dowel first, then introduce the saw to the wire. Allow the links to fall as they are cut, collecting them in a drawer, a towel, or box in your lap.

TIP
Alternately, links can be cut using an abrasive cut off wheel on the flex shaft. This leaves a sharp bur which often needs to be sanded or filed off.

Opening and Closing Links

In order to make a chain, you will need to learn to open and close the links properly. Using flat-nosed pliers for this job will keep from cutting or marring the wire. Grab each end of the wire at the opening of the link with a pair of pliers. To open link, twist the wire ends from side to side to create a gap. Never open the link by pulling the ends of the circle apart because it is almost impossible to get the link back into a round shape once it has been opened this way. To close the link, simply twist the ends back into place.

CAUTION

Never polish chains on the polishing wheel. Polish by hand with a polishing cloth. A chain could become wrapped around the shaft of the motor and could potentially cause harm.

Bezel Settings

A bezel is a thin metal wall that holds a stone in place. Very thin metal is used that can be formed to the shape of the stone. Most silver bezels are made from fine silver as it is much softer than sterling silver and easier to form around the stone. Stones are the very last pieces to be added to the work since most cannot withstand the heat of soldering. Bezel wire is available from most metal suppliers, or can be rolled down from thicker material in the rolling mill. Most bezel wire is between 24 and 30-gauge. A bezel can be very plain or decorated to become ornate, depending on your style.

Bezels are most always used to hold cabochons, which are stones with a rounded cross section. Bezels can also be used with faceted stones instead of traditional prong settings. Here, the bezel holds this stone that has been fashioned into a ring.

You will need

- Bezel wire
- Stone to be set
- Jeweler's saw frame
- Saw blades
- Pliers
- Emery paper
- Burnishing tool
- Files
- Firebrick
- Flux & brush
- Solder
- Torch
- Tweezers
- Striker
- Bowl with water
- Copper tongs
- Pickle & pickle pot

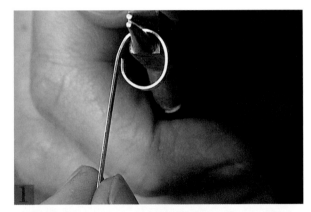

Step 1

Cut bezel wire to desired height for your stone. This should be tall enough to grasp the stone, but not so tall as to obscure it. When in doubt, make it taller, it can always be sanded down. Use pliers to bend the wire to the approximate shape of the stone being used.

Step 2

Fit the bezel wire directly around the stone and mark where the joint would be. The wire should fit snugly around the stone.

Step 3

Using a jeweler's saw with a fine blade, cut the bezel wire to the length needed. Cut the ends square. Flux and solder the bezel wire ends together using medium or hard solder. Quench and pickle. When in doubt, make the bezel wire slightly smaller and hammer it lightly to stretch if needed. A bezel that is too big will need to be cut apart and re-soldered. Place the bezel around the stone and test the fit. Adjust as needed.

Step 4

Sand the bezel bottom edge to ensure that it is perfectly flat. Re-check the shape of bezel to stone and test to make certain that the stone can be dropped in from above. Do not force the stone into the bezel as this will make it difficult to remove.

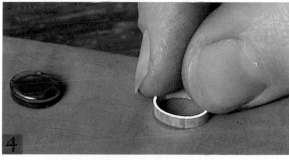

Step 5

Prepare a piece of metal that will be the base piece of the bezel setting. Cut a piece of sheet metal that is a little larger than the bezel setting. It is always easier to solder to a slightly larger piece of metal and file it down to size after soldering.

Continued on next page

Bezel Settings

Step 6

Flux and place the solder chips flat on the metal just touching the inside edge of the bezel. Heat from underneath to help draw the solder around the edge of the bezel wire. Heating from above will often cause the thin bezel wire to heat prematurely and melt. Air cool and pickle. Using a jeweler's saw, cut the sheet metal around the bezel to desired shape. File and sand.

Step 7

Very gently and carefully test fit the stone, never pushing it into place until you are certain that it is ready to be set. You may need to use a burnishing tool to slightly bend the bezel away from the edge to allow for test fitting of the stone. When you are satisfied with the fit, and the piece is fully polished, ease the stone into place.

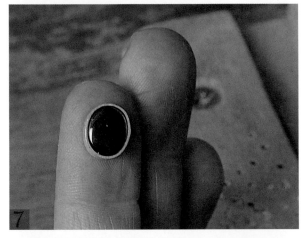

Step 8

Using the burnishing tool, begin pushing the edge of the metal bezel over the stone. Work slowly around the stone and continually check the height of the bezel. Avoid pushing too much in one area as it can create wrinkles in the bezel. Continue burnishing until the stone is securely set.

Fitting Hint

When test fitting the stone, check the top edge of the bezel with the stone to make sure it is the proper height. The bezel should grip the stone securely but not be so tall that it obscures the stone. If it is too high, remove stone and sand the top edge if needed.

TIPS

• Methods for removing stuck stones include using tape to help assist pulling, sharply hitting the work with a block of wood while holding the work in your hand, or drilling a hole in the reverse to push the stone out of the bezel.

• Do not sand the bezel while the stone is in place as most emery paper will scratch stones. Instead, use a soft abrasive wheel on the flex shaft to polish out any scratches. Tiny buffs will help bring the work to shiny perfection.

• With practice you can achieve the ideal look. Repeating the process will yield stunning results.

Reticulation

A controlled melting called reticulation produces an abstract pattern on the surface of metal. It is never exactly the same twice, but you can develop techniques to reproduce similar patterns in subsequent projects. It is a wise idea to practice melting on scrap metal to experience the process rather than having it accidentally happen while a piece is being soldered. A valuable lesson to learn is the subtle nuances between soldering and melting.

You will need
- Reticulation silver or an alloy close to 80% silver and 20% copper, high karat gold, or brass
- Firebrick
- Torch
- Bowl of water
- Pickle & pickle pot
- Brass brush

Step 1

Place the metal sheet on firebrick. Heat the metal sheet to its annealing point. Quench in water and then place in pickle solution. This pickle will remove the copper oxide from the surface. Rinse in warm water. Lightly scour the surface with a brass brush and then dry. The material will appear very white and dull with this layer of fine silver on the surface.Repeat this process of heating and pickle until no copper comes to the surface, as many as 8 to 10 times. The material will be a sandwich of layers of pure silver on the exterior with the more or less 80/20-alloy in-between them.

Sections of reticulated metal were cut into disk shapes and fabricated into a ring and a pendant. The reticulated metal was oxidized to accentuate the pattern.

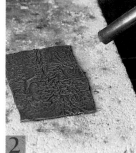

Step 2

Place the metal piece on a clean firebrick and begin heating with a torch, using a bushy flame. Move the torch over the surface until the metal begins to melt and buckle. Continue until you achieve an interesting pattern. The distance of the torch from the metal as well as the movement and angle of the torch will affect the resulting texture. Reticulate a fairly large area of the metal so that you can choose a section of the pattern that you like best for a particular piece of jewelry. Allow the metal to cool then place in pickle solution.

TIP
To remove the dull layer and regain the silver shine, scrub the metal piece with a brass brush.

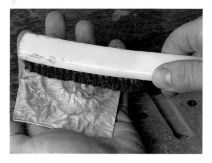

The Chemical Reaction

Reticulation relies on repeated heating of the metal to produce a heavy oxide layer on a piece of metal. With reticulation silver (also called coin silver), this oxide layer is copper, which bonds with oxygen quickly when heated. This is also why sterling silver tarnishes or oxidizes slowly over time. The copper in the sterling alloy is bonding with the oxygen in the air we breathe to create a thin oxide layer that we call tarnish. In reticulation, the copper oxide layer is created by heating, and then stripped away in the pickle solution. Left behind is a layer of pure silver. The outer and inner layers have different melting points and different rates of expansion; this is what causes the wrinkling and buckling characteristic of reticulation when the entire work is heated nearly to its melting point.

Soldering

In jewelry-making, soldering is the way pieces are most often joined together. Soldering is a skill that will require learning the basics and practicing the skill many times to become proficient. Because soldering involves heat and gas under pressure, read the cautions carefully and practice them. One important rule to remember is to heat the metal evenly and not overheat it to the point of melting it completely

You will need

- Metal pieces to be joined
- Firebrick
- Flux & brush
- Solder
- Tweezers
- Torch
- Striker
- Bowl with water
- Copper tongs
- Pickle & pickle pot

Step 1

Place the metal pieces on the firebrick. Using a small brush, apply flux in a thin layer to the areas of the pieces to be soldered together. Flux only the area where you are soldering because the solder will flow only on the fluxed areas. Allow flux to dry.

Photo 1—The stem is being soldered to the gingko leaf piece. Notice there is a small chip of solder between the two pieces.

Photo 2—The cooled piece is put into the pickle pot for a few minutes to remove flux and any oxides that may occur.

Step 2

Prepare your solder. Cut tiny pieces from solder wire or sheet. Using tweezers, place the solder in the area to be joined. After creating a few pieces of soldered jewelry you will learn how much solder to use and where to place it. Too little solder is better than too much as more solder can be added if needed. Removing excess solder is almost always difficult and produces undesirable scratches if not completed with extreme care.

Step 3

Light the torch with the striker. Hold the torch with one hand and the tweezers with the dominate hand. With the metal still on the firebrick, heat the entire piece evenly, moving the torch with a circular motion around the work. The entire piece and the solder should reach the same temperature at the same time. Heat until the solder melts and flows into the joint (see photo 1). Remove the flame. Pick up the piece and quench in cold water. Alternately, you can let it air cool.

Step 4

Place the cooled piece in the pickle pot for a few minutes (see photo 2). Remove and rinse under cold running water.

Pieces of metal wire will form a frame. The first two corners are soldered together using hard solder.

The next two corners are soldered together using medium solder. Medium solder flows at a lower melting point, assuring that the first two solders will not re-melt.

Rules for Soldering

1. **Good fit.** Solder will not fill gaps, so a perfect fit is necessary.

2. **Clean work.** Solder does not like to adhere to work that is dirty. Have the metal pieces sanded to a clean finish and free of fingerprints.

3. **Enough flux.** Use enough that it won't burn off, but not so much that it bubbles up and causes the solder to move around.

4. **Even heat.** The entire work must come up to the melting temperature to solder evenly. A torch positioned on just one part of the metal will cause it to heat and usually melt before the solder does.

5. **Work quickly.** Once the solder has begun to flow, remove the heat source. Do not overheat the metal. If the metal is beginning to glow red or orange, it is telling you that it is ready to melt.

6. **Solder likes heat.** The solder will tend to flow towards the heat source. Use this to your advantage to draw solder into a seam with the position of the torch.

Direct Casting

Most of the techniques previously described in this book are fabrication methods. Sheet, wire, and other types of metal are cut and formed and soldered together to form the finished jewelry. Casting differs tremendously from fabrication in the process of creating jewelry in metal. Casting is the technique of pouring molten metal into a special encased mold that will withstand extremely high temperatures.

There are two types of casting I will introduce here: direct casting and lost wax casting. For any type of casting, a mold must be used. Direct casting is an easy, low-tech casting method to try before attempting lost wax casting.

Direct casting involves pouring molten metal directly into a prepared heat-resistant mold. I like to make heat-proof molds by carving into cuttlefish bones. Cuttlefish bone is a calcium rich endoskeleton of a squid-like creature that lives at the bottom of the ocean. It has a delicate pattern much like wood grain or patterns reminiscent of fingerprints, windswept snow or sand, and topographical maps.

These beautifully textured earrings and pendant were cast in a cuttlefish bone mold.

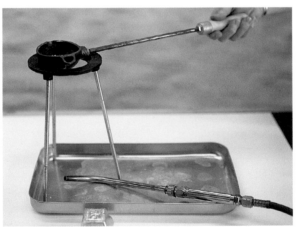

Pictured: crucible, torch, metal tray, pewter

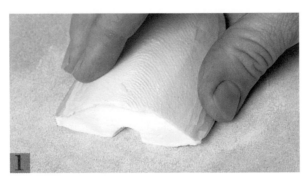

You will need
- Metal for casting, pewter is preferred
- Cuttlefish bone
- Jeweler's saw
- Sandpaper, 100 to 200 grit
- Carving tools (for clay) or dental tools
- Small paintbrush
- Duct tape or steel binding wire
- Coffee can or metal tray
- Crucible (different one for each metal you use)
- Charcoal block or firebrick
- Water in bowl
- Tweezers

CAUTION
Contamination warning: Keep tools used for pewter separate from other tools. Small bits of pewter can contaminate silver and other metals, so keep a set of tools and preferably a work area separate for pewter work.

Step 1
To create the mold, you will need to prepare the cuttlefish bone by removing one or both ends with a saw. If the bone is large, cut it in half crosswise. With the soft side down, rub on sandpaper to create a flat surface.

Step 2

Use a carving tool or scribe to create a funnel in one end of the bone. This will be the opening for pouring in the molten metal. Make it an actual funnel shape, large enough at the top to accept the molten metal, and tapering at bottom so metal will not enter mold too quickly.

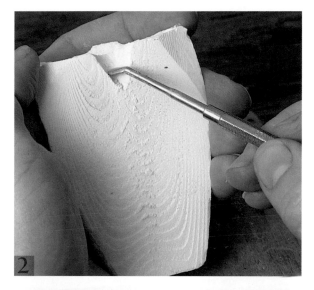

Step 3

At the bottom of this funnel, begin carving a design of your choice. In general, keep designs within a $1/2$ inch (13 mm) of the perimeter of the bone. Do not carve too deeply, and make designs trail downward from the funnel. Molten metal does not like to travel upwards, so a little planning in advance can make a better casting just by orienting the design well. Use a small brush to remove all dust from the cavity and to help expose the grain in the cuttlefish.

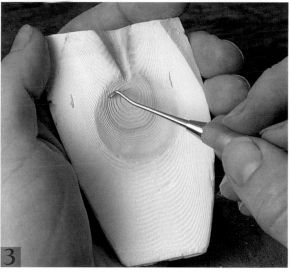

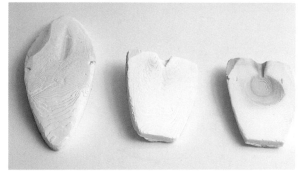

This shows the progression of the carving to make the cuttlefish mold for the pendant.

Direct Casting

Step 4

Press the cuttlefish bone against a charcoal block or a firebrick. The carved area will be encased. Hold this up to the light to see if any cracks are visible between the cuttlefish and the charcoal block or firebrick. Molten metal will find the tiniest crevice to escape. If any light can be seen, sand the cuttlefish lightly to make the surface absolutely flat. Use wire or duct tape to secure the mold to the firebrick. Duct tape is sufficient for low temperature melting metals such as pewter. For silver and brass, use steel binding wire.

Step 5

To prepare for pouring the molten metal into the mold, place mold in a coffee can or on a metal tray. This will be the surface where the mold will rest while pouring. Use only non-combustible materials and prop up the mold so that it won't tip or fall. Heat pewter in a cast iron crucible from underneath using a torch. Heat until the metal is molten—do not overheat or allow it to smoke. Extinguish the flame on the torch.

Step 6

Immediately pour the metal slowly and carefully into the cuttlefish mold.

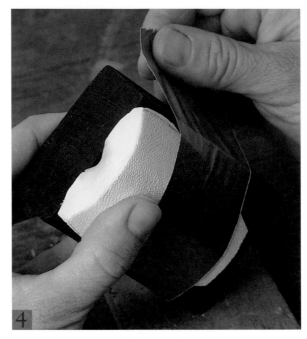

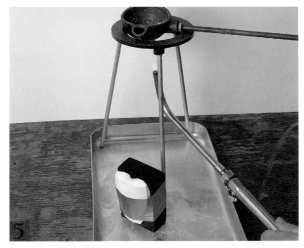

CAUTIONS

- Do not attempt casting if you are not properly informed. This process can be extremely dangerous if approached recklessly.

- Molten metal is extremely hot. The melting points of several metals are well above 1,000° Fahrenheit (537° C).

- Always wear protective eyewear, heat proof gloves, and protective clothing.

- Work on a dry and fireproof surface.

- Crucible and working areas must be totally dry. Molten metal and water do not mix. If molten metal gets in contact with water it is likely to explode, splashing hot metal everywhere.

- Never look directly into a high-powered flame.

Step 7

Allow mold to cool for three to five minutes. Metal will harden and the firebrick will become cool enough to handle. Remove tape or wire carefully from the mold to expose the cast piece.

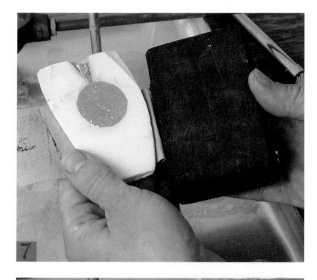

Step 8

Use tweezers to remove casting from cuttlefish mold. Quench metal in a cup of cool water.

TIP

Careful extraction of the casting from the mold can allow for multiple castings from one mold.

Finishing

Using a jeweler's saw, cut off the cast area of the funnel. Alternately, shape the funnel cast area into a bail for pendants, or a stand for small sculptures. File, sand, and polish as needed. Finish as desired by adding findings of your choice to create jewelry.

Lost Wax Casting

One of the most common methods that jeweler's use to mold pieces is called lost wax casting. In a nutshell, this involves making a wax model, surrounding that in a plaster-like substance called investment, and then melting the wax out of the investment to create the mold. Molten metal is then poured into the cavity of the mold.

For this method you will design a model for your jewelry piece using jeweler's casting wax. The wax model is used to make the mold into which the molten metal will be poured. This casting method is much more advanced than the direct casting method. Creating models in wax is an art form in itself.

Carving Hints

Carving hard wax is a subtractive process that involves carving areas away from a larger block. Using soft wax is an additive process of building up areas and joining bits of wax together. Hard waxes are available in different types/colors that range from hard to flexible. Hard wax is usually available in blocks or sheets or hollow extruded tubes convenient for creating rings. Soft wax is available in sheet and wire shapes and is easily manipulated with a little warm water, the heat from your hands, or tools heated with an alcohol lamp. Both waxes can be used.

A hammer and anvil were cast in silver using the lost wax casting method.

Pictured: wax types for carving models. The rods are the sprue wax. The rectangular pieces and tube pieces are hard carving wax, and the sheet is soft wax. Jewelers use soft and hard waxes specifically made for casting. Any wax will work but these specialty waxes have been designed especially for jewelers.

You will need

All of these supplies are especially made for the lost wax casting process. You can find them where fine jewelry-making supplies are sold.

- Hard and soft carving wax
- Sprue wax
- Wax carving tools
- Spiral saw blades
- Alcohol lamp for melting carving wax
- Denatured alcohol for lamp
- Casting flask
- Rubber sprue base
- Investment
- Rubber mixing bowl
- Centrifugal casting machine
- Crucible for metal
- Casting metal, sterling casting grains used
- Burnout kiln

Carving Tools

A variety of tools can be used to carve your design into the wax: wax files, spiral saw blades designed for sawing wax, and specialty flexible shaft tools designed for use with hard wax. Tools for working with soft wax include specialty wax tools, dental picks, and wax pens which extrude varying amounts of wax at different temperatures.

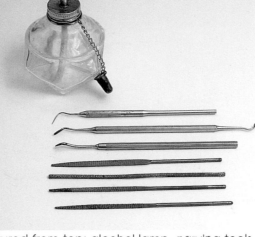

Pictured from top: alcohol lamp, carving tools, needle files

Casting Process Supplies

The flask, when sealed at the bottom with the rubber base, will hold the plaster-like investment to create the mold. The rubber mixing bowl is used to mix the investment material.

Pictured clockwise from left: tongs, flask, rubber mixing bowl, sterling silver casting grains in crucible, rubber base

CAUTIONS

• Casting involves working with molten metal. Molten metal is extremely hot. The melting points of several metals are well above 1,000° Fahrenheit (537° C).

• Take proper precautions when working with molten metal. This process can be extremely dangerous if approached recklessly or if you are not properly informed.

• Always wear protective eyewear, heat proof gloves, and protective clothing.

• Work on a dry and fireproof surface.

• The crucible and working areas must be totally dry. Molten metal and water do not mix. If molten metal gets in contact with water, it is likely to explode, splashing hot metal everywhere.

• Never look directly into a high-powered flame.

Lost Wax Casting

Create the Wax Model

Create your design by first making a model using casting wax. It can be as simple as a geometric shape or as detailed as the hammer and anvil shown in the example.

Step 1

Transfer and scribe the jewelry design into the wax. Any type of pointed carving tool can be used for this. Draw the basic outline of the design into the wax.

Step 2

Cut away some of the wax to rough out the design using a saw or files. Wax files are coarse toothed files that will ease the roughing out of shapes.

Step 3

After roughing out the design, use carving tools and more fine files to refine shapes. Wax can be taken down to a very fine surface so that minimal work will need to be completed once the wax is cast into metal. Everything in wax will be translated in metal, so take time while working to finish surfaces as much as possible. A little time refining a wax model can save a lot of time in refining the surface of a cast piece.

Inspiration for Jewelry Designs

You may not think sculpting is your thing. But you will be surprised how easy it is once you tackle the process. Start by carving out a simple geometric shape from the wax. A shape as simple as a cube can be a start. After you have carved the cube from the block of wax, carve out some dots on each side to create a die, make two and you have a pair of dice. After you have cast the pieces, adding patina will make the dots black, enhancing the look of the dice. Use them as earrings or charms. Thinking in three dimensions will take some getting used to. Use game pieces, children's small plastic toys, or everyday tools for some inspiration.

TIP

Spiral saw blades aid in cutting wax. They can be a little difficult to control as they cut on all sides. Always cut a bit wider than the planned form to allow for clean up with a file.

Attach a Sprue to Carved Wax Model

Sprues are tube-like pieces of 8-gauge sprue wax that are added to the carved model. The sprue acts as a channel for the wax to escape when being burned out from the investment mold. The channel that is created in the mold by the sprue allows the metal to get into the void of the mold. The sprues should be attached to heaviest part of the casting and in an area where they can be easily removed from the finished casting. It is important to add enough sprues that are correctly placed to deliver the metal so that it can flow as easily as possible, without making sharp bends or attempting to flow upwards. The metal will not flow easily through very thin sections so place sprues adjacent to such places.

Step 4

To prepare for attaching the sprue to the carved wax design, heat the end of the sprue wax piece on the alcohol burner.

Step 5

Push the sprue piece onto the carved design. Hold in place until it has set.

Step 6

Pinch off the excess sprue wax. The sprue piece should be about 1/2 inch (13 mm) to 1 inch (26 mm).

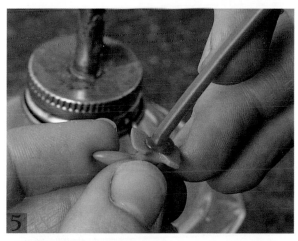

TIP

Remember that every detail will show in your cast piece, so make the wax model as refined as possible. Refine the connection of the sprue to the carved piece using a carving tool or dental tool that has been heated on the alcohol lamp.

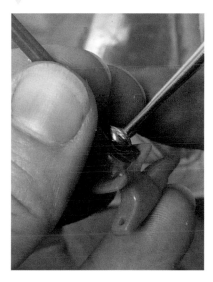

Lost Wax Casting

Make the Investment Mold

Step 7

The wax model will next be attached to a rubber base. Heat the end of the sprue with the alcohol lamp to soften the wax. Push the sprue onto the rubber sprue base. This rubber base keeps the sprue in place while the investment sets up and acts as a tight seal around the bottom of the metal flask. Take care to make a smooth transition between the sprue base and the sprue to allow the metal to flow as smoothly as possible.

Step 8

Place the metal flask onto the rubber base. This flask will contain the investment mold during the burnout process and during the casting process.

Step 9

Pour the investment solution into the flask. Work quickly as the investment will set after ten minutes of mixing, but do not work too quickly because investment that is poured too soon will leave a watery area at the top of the flask. To keep air bubbles from forming in the investment, pour it over the back side of a spoon or a palette knife into the flask. Then tap the side of the flask with that same spoon to facilitate the movement of the bubbles to the surface.

Allow the investment to cure for at least 30 minutes. When the investment is set, remove the rubber base. Wait at least two more hours before beginning the burnout of the wax from the mold, but not more than 24 hours or the investment can dry out too much.

Mixing the Investment

Investment is a plaster-like substance that can withstand the extreme heat of the kiln and the metal. It is available in powdered form and mixed with water, then poured into a metal flask. Mix enough investment using a wooden stick or a palette knife to fill the flask. Determining how much investment to mix is a tricky process. With the rubber sprue base on the flask and the wax inside, fill the flask two thirds full with water. Pour the water into a rubber mixing bowl and add investment powder, stirring constantly. Continue to mix investment until it reaches the consistency of pudding.

Begin Wax Burnout

Burnout is the term for removing the wax from the investment mold. It involves the heating of the flask and the investment to remove the wax, leaving a cavity into which the metal will be cast.

Step 10

Place the flask filled with the hardened investment into the kiln. Support the flask with a wire or ceramic frame that allows all of the wax to drip out of the opening that faces downwards. This opening is the area where the spruc was attached. Burnout for the first hour at 150° Fahrenheit (65.5° C), then gradually increase the temperature over the next one to two hours until it reaches between 1000-1200° Fahrenheit (537-648° C). Increase the temperature of the kiln to close to the melting point of the metal. At these high temperatures the wax will melt out and be completely vaporized. Make certain that you have a hood and ventilation system to exhaust the fumes outside. It is also possible to catch the wax in a pan and remove it before increasing the heat. This will reduce the mess and fumes from burnout.

Cast the Metal

This example uses the centrifugal casting technique.

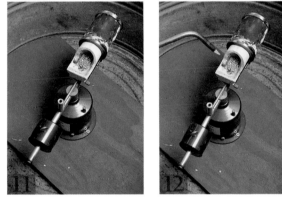

How much metal will I need?

First weigh the carved wax model on a scale. By using the adjacent chart for the specific gravity of the metal to be cast, it is easy to determine the amount of metal needed by multiplying the weight of the wax by the factor of the metal. It is necessary to add additional metal for the *button* where the sprue is attached to the sprue base. Generally this is half again the weight of the sprue and wax to make certain there is enough metal for the casting. Usually jewelers weigh items in pennyweights abbreviated as dwt. Any unit of measure is acceptable as long as it is consistent.

Wax weight x specific gravity = metal required for casting
Specific Gravity
Sterling—11
14 karat gold—14
18 karat gold—15.5

Step 11

When using the centrifuge, wind the machine three turns and use the locking pin to secure it in place. Pour metal casting grains into the crucible. Wearing heat proof gloves and using tongs, remove the flask from the kiln and place the flask in the cradle of the centrifuge.

Step 12

Heat the metal with a torch using a bushy reducing flame. Sprinkle the metal with powdered borax halfway through the melting and continue to heat until the metal is molten. This will prevent oxides from building up on the metal. Heat the metal until it is fluid. Do not overheat the metal as this can lead to porosity in the casting. Pull the locking pin from the centrifuge and let the machine spin until it comes to a stop.

Remove the flask with tongs. While holding the flask horizontally, plunge it into a bucket of water. It will rumble and then usually pop as the investment and the metal are cooled quickly by the water. Search the water for the casting. Clean the investment from your casting and the inside of the flask. Never pour investment down the drain, but allow the solids to settle in the bucket and pour off the water, disposing of the investment in the trash. File, sand, and polish the casting as desired.

CHAPTER 4

Projects

Now that you have been introduced to the essential techniques of metal smithing, you might like to try creating some jewelry pieces. Use the ideas and instructions here to hone your skills. Before long you will be creating your own jewelry designs.

Refer to the *Tools & Supplies* and the *Techniques* chapters as needed for detailed information on each fabricating procedure.

63

Sailor's Chain

This is a sturdy chain, also known as a pinched loop chain. This chain is used to hold a pocket watch. It contains 37 links. At one end of the link I attached a watch clasp. At the other end, I fabricated a decorative loop from silver wire. Hammering the links gives the chain great texture and flair, catching and reflecting the light. Make it longer to be worn as a necklace or shorter for a bracelet.

You will need

- 18-gauge silver wire
- Wood dowel, ½ inch (13 mm) diameter
- Jeweler's saw & blades
- Soldering supplies
- 2 metal rods, each ³⁄₁₆ inch (5 mm) diameter
- 1 metal rod, ³⁄₃₂ inch (2 mm) diameter
- 1 metal rod, ⅛ inch (3 mm) diameter
- Bench vise
- Round-nosed pliers, two pair
- Cross peen hammer
- Round-faced hammer
- Steel block
- Polishing compound
- Polishing cloth

Here's How

Please see the *Techniques* chapter for detailed information on making links and forging.

Make Links

1. Wrap the silver wire around the wood dowel to make each link. Wrap the wire around dowel in a coil 37 times to make 37 links. Make a few extra wraps in case of mistakes.

2. Using a jeweler's saw, cut crosswise across the coil to create individual links. Remove the links from the dowel.

3. Solder each link closed using medium silver solder. Pickle. Rinse.

Shape Links

4. Insert the two 3/16-inch (5 mm) metal rods into one of the links. Pull each rod outward to form the link into an oval shape (see photo 1). Do not over stretch the links beyond just giving them form.

5. Bend the oval link evenly in half over the 3/32-inch (2 mm) metal rod (see photo 2). Remove link from rod.

6. Insert a 1/8-inch (3 mm) metal rod vertically in the bench vise. Place the link over this rod with the wide end of the loops touching the rod. Insert a 3/32-inch (2 mm) rod horizontally in the smaller end of the loops (see photo 3).

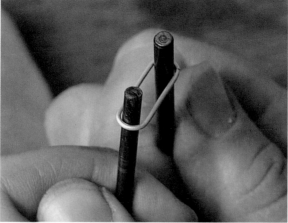
Photo 1

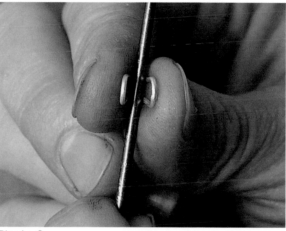
Photo 2

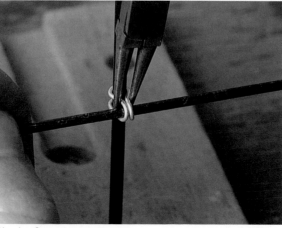
Photo 3

Sailor's Chain

7. Holding the ³/₃₂-inch (2mm) rod with one hand, use the other hand to hold round-nosed pliers to pinch the loops both vertically and horizontally around the metal rods to give the loop form (see photo 3).

Texture Links

8. Open out the wide end of the link slightly using two pair of pliers (see photo 4). You will do this so you can work on each end of the loop to texture it.

9. Use a round-faced hammer to flatten both sides of the link (see photo 5).

10. Texture the link using a very small cross peen hammer. Make direct blows to radiate from the center outward of the wide loop (see photo 6).

Create Chain

11. Gently close the loop around the ³/₃₂-inch (2 mm) rod (see photo 7).

12. Weave the links together by putting the large end of the link through the smaller end of the next link. Repeat until desired length is achieved. Adjust links with pliers as necessary while adding links to the chain.

13. Polish lightly if needed with polishing compound and a polishing cloth.

Photo 4

Photo 5

Photo 6

Photo 7

Lots of Links Chain

The name "Idiot's Delight" is often given to this technique. This chain looks difficult, but it is quite easy. It is merely made of double sets of links attached to one another in an unusual way. A beautiful clasp was fashioned from forged metal.

You will need
- 18-gauge silver wire
- 14-gauge silver wire
- Wood dowel, 5/32 inch (4 mm) diameter
- Jeweler's saw
- Wire
- Planishing hammer
- Steel block
- Files
- Polishing compound
- Polishing cloth

Here's How

Please see the *Techniques* chapter for detailed information on making links and forging.

Make Links

1. Wrap the 18-gauge wire around the wooden dowel to make as many links as needed.

2. Use a jeweler's saw to cut a large number of links. You can cut more as needed.

Create Necklace

3. Stack two open links, one on top of the other. Slide four closed links onto the set of two stacked links. Close the two open links. Separate the links into two-link sets. The result will be a three-link chain of double links. Secure the first two links with in a piece of wire to a bench or work surface to act as an anchor (see fig. 1).

4. Fold back the last two links (links 5 & 6), placing one on each side of the chain (see fig. 2).

5. Push links 5&6 forward in order to spread links 3 & 4 and create a space between them. Links 5 & 6 are now peeking out between links 3 & 4 (see fig. 3).

6. Attach two links to links 5 & 6 in the space between links 3 & 4 (see fig. 4).

7. Attach two more links to links 7 & 8.

8. Repeat steps 4 through 7 to continue the pattern. Add links until you have make the length of chain desired for your necklace.

Forge Clasp

9. To make the clasp, first form the 14-gauge wire into an "S" hook shape. Use the photo of the clasp as a pattern. This photo shows the clasp at actual size. Place the shaped wire on a steel block and forge it with a planishing hammer to flatten. File as needed to shape the ends. Hook the clasp onto the end links of the chain.

10. Polish to the desired shine.

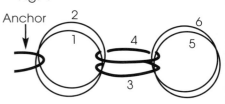

Fig. 1

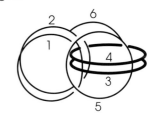

Fig. 2

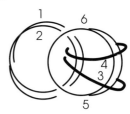

Fig. 3

Fig. 4

Egyptian Spiral Bracelet

Twist silver wire to create a design that looks like a fancy monogram. Solder silver snake chain, in the same diameter as the silver wire, to the formed wire design to create a necklace. Have fun creating a design of your choice.

You will need
- 18-gauge silver wire
- Fine tip marker
- Pliers
- Wire cutters
- Polishing compound
- Polishing cloth
- Clasp

Here's How
Please see the *Techniques* chapter for detailed information on working with wire and making links and forging.

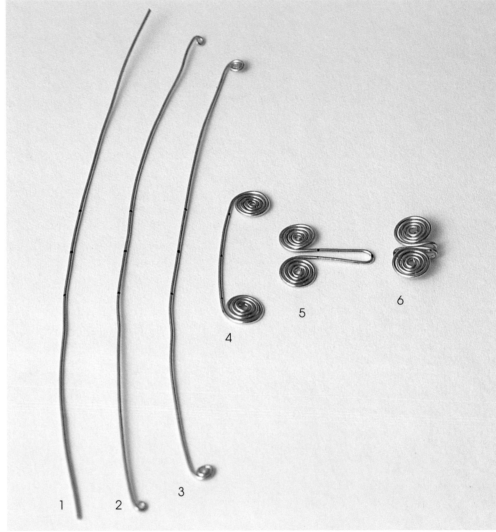

Stages of making the links

Make Links
1. Using wire cutters, cut wire into 3-inch long (75 mm) pieces. Cut 21 pieces.

2. Mark the center point of each wire piece using the fine tip marker.

Form Links
3. Roll tight spirals on the two ends of each wire piece, 1/4 inch (6 mm) diameter each. Roll the ends of the wire towards the center, rolling one end clockwise and the other end counter clockwise. (See the fourth stage in the *Stages* photo.)

4. Bend the wire in the center with spirals facing away from each other. (See the fifth stage in the *Stages* photo.)

5. Bend the center section down over itself to form a loop. (See the sixth stage in the *Stages* photo.)

Make Necklace
6. Assemble the chain by sliding one center loop through the preceding loop.

7. Polish necklace.

8. Add clasp.

Spiral Wire Rings

Silver wire is fun to shape. These wire rings are super easy to make. Use your creativity to form a variety of geometric shapes for ring decoration.

You will need
- 10 or 12-gauge wire
- Wire cutters
- Planishing hammer
- File
- Round-nosed pliers
- Ring mandrel
- Polishing compound
- Polishing cloth

Here's How

Please see the *Techniques* chapter for detailed information on working with wire.

1. Cut wire to roughly 6 inches (15 cm) long or more, depending on design and the size of ring needed.

2. File the ends of each piece to a taper using a file (see photo 1A).

3. Bend ends into a spiral or desired shape using round-nosed pliers (see photo 1B & C). Avoid excessive force that will make marks on wire that need to be removed.

4. Bend the shank of the ring around a ring mandrel to desired size (see photo 2).

5. Hammer the metal to work harden and add sparkle to the ring (see photo 3).

6. Polish ring.

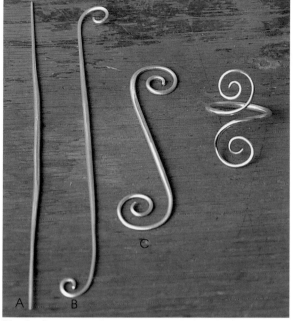

Photo 1

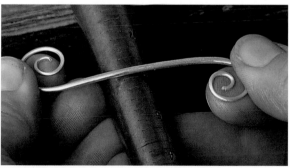

Photo 2

Photo 3

Wirework Pendant

Silver wire is twisted to create a design that looks like a fancy monogram. Have fun creating a design of your choice. Silver snake chain in the same diameter of the silver wire is soldered to the formed wire design to create a necklace.

You will need
- 16-gauge silver wire
- Wire cutters
- Emery paper
- Round nose pliers
- Soldering supplies, and easy solder
- Polishing compound
- Polishing cloth
- Snake chain, 16-gauge

Here's How
Please see the *Techniques* chapter for detailed information on working with wire.

1. Cut a piece of silver wire 10 inches (25.5 cm) long.

2. File both ends to a taper using emery paper.

3. Bend ends in opposite directions, creating a small spiral in one end and a shepherd's hook in the other end.

4. Begin with the spiral end to form the small figure-eight shape.

5. Continue twisting the wire, passing it under the spiral end and back around towards the end with the shepherd's hook.

6. Attach the snake chain to the pendant with easy solder.

7. Polish by hand.

Coil Links Bracelet

Wire coils are formed then linked together to form a bracelet. Sawing multiple links, fusing or soldering them together, and then forming and joining those links allow a metalsmith ample opportunity to hone fabrication skills.

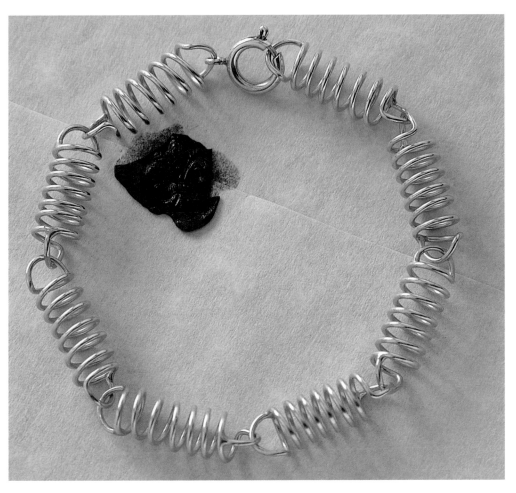

You will need

- 18-gauge wire
- Spring clasp
- Wood dowel, $1/4$ inch (6 mm) diameter
- Permanent fine tip marker
- Wire cutters
- Round-nosed pliers
- Soldering supplies
- Polishing compound
- Polishing cloth

Here's How

See *Making Links* in the *Techniques* chapter for detailed information.

1. Wrap the wire around the length of your wood dowel.

2. Count links and use a fine point marker to make marks every sixth coil.

3. Cut the links at the marks using wire cutters. This should result in wire coil units that have six coils each. Make as many coiled units as needed to create the bracelet size to fit your wrist, or enough for a necklace length.

4. Holding a link in one hand, use pliers to bend one half of the end link up at a 90° angle to the coil. Repeat on the other end.

5. Attach links to one another, using pliers to bend and form attachment.

6. Solder links closed using a very fine point torch tip.

7. Polish to shine desired.

8. Attach a spring clasp to one end of bracelet.

Forged Earrings with Pearls

Using a forging technique, you can quickly create stunning earrings. A beautiful freshwater pearl is just the right touch to add sophistication to this earring set.

You will need

- Sterling silver wire, 2 mm square
- 2 freshwater pewter pearls, 8 mm each
- 22-gauge silver wire
- Jeweler's saw
- Cross peen hammer
- Steel block
- Pickle & pickle pot
- Soldering supplies
- Stud earring findings
- Emery paper, 200 to 600 grit
- Polishing compound, bobbing and white diamond
- Buffing machine and buffing wheels

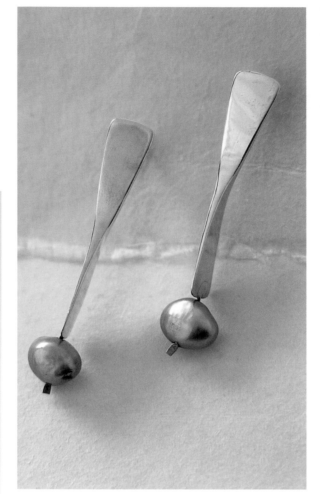

Here's How

Please see the *Techniques* chapter for detailed information on forging, soldering, and buffing.

Forge the Metal

1. For each earring, cut a piece of sterling wire approximately 1½ inches (4 cm) long using a jeweler's saw.

2. Anneal and pickle each piece. Dry thoroughly.

3. Using a cross peen hammer, strike the end of the square wire lengthwise. Keep hammer strokes even and pay close attention so that the metal forges out symmetrically left to right in a fan shape. Correct as needed with a file or adjust hammer blows if shape becomes asymmetrical. Work on a steel block with a rounded edge to prevent making marks in the cross peen hammer (see photo 1).

4. With the end of the metal close to the edge of the steel block, slowly angle hammer marks to spread out the end of the metal in a fan-like shape.

5. Turn the silver piece end-for-end and then rotate one-quarter turn.

6. Forge this opposite end in the same manner, working until it reaches the same shape as the first end. Forge until the metal does not move. (Photo 2 shows the stages of the forging)

7. Anneal and repeat steps 4 through 6 until desired shape is achieved. Usually this takes three courses of hammering and annealing.

Finish

8. Attach a pre-made earring stud on the back of each piece using medium solder.

9. On each earring, attach a 1/2-inch (13 mm) piece of 22-gauge wire to the end that is opposite the earring stud.

10. To achieve a high polished finish, sand with emery paper. Start with 200 grit, using finer grit until you finish with 600 grit. Then polish piece on the buffer with bobbing compound, followed by white diamond compound to get an ultra-high sheen.

11. Add a pearl to each earring on the 1/2-inch (13 mm) piece of wire. Use a small tool to spread the end of the wire to keep the pearl attached.

Photo 1

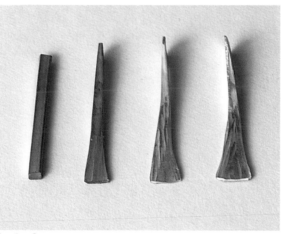
Photo 2

Forged Wire Drop Earrings

Silver wire and pearls make lovely dangling earrings. So easy yet so elegant.

You will need

- 18-gauge silver wire
- 6 freshwater pewter pearls, 8 mm each
- Stud and ball earring findings with eye
- Cross peen hammer
- Wire cutters
- Pliers, flat-nosed

Here's How

Please see the *Techniques* chapter for detailed information on forging.

1. Snip two pieces of wire, each 3¹/₂ inches (9 cm) long.

2. Cut two more pieces of wire, each 2¹/₂ inches (6.5 cm) long.

3. Cut two more pieces of wire, each 1¹/₂ inches (3.8 cm) long.

4. Slide a pearl onto each piece of wire.

5. Working with one piece of wire at a time, slide pearl up the wire to the top. Use the cross peen hammer to flatten out each bottom end of the wire pieces into a

slight fan shape. This will keep the pearl from sliding off the end of the wire. Slide pearl back down until it stops.

6. Bend an eye on the end of each piece of wire. Attach three of the pearl/wire pieces, each of a different length, to the loop of the earring stud. Using pliers, close wire eyes around the loop of stud.

Textured Copper Earrings

Copper is easy to work with and more inexpensive than silver or gold. These earrings would make a good beginner project.

You will need

- 18-gauge copper sheet metal
- 2 metallic freshwater pearls, 5 mm each
- 20-gauge silver wire
- Tracing paper, cardstock, pencil, scissors
- Scribe
- Snips
- Jeweler's saw
- Texturing hammer
- Steel block
- Soldering supplies, easy solder
- Liver of sulfur
- Polishing cloth

Here's How

1. A pattern is included for the shape of these earrings. Trace the shape onto cardstock and cut out. Place the cardstock pattern onto the metal and trace around it with a scribe to mark the pattern for cutting.

2. Cut out the earring shapes using a jeweler's saw.

3. Texture the metal using consistent blows with the texturing hammer. File and sand edges to smooth.

4. Cut two pieces of wire, each 3 inches (76 mm) long to make the ear wires.

5. Position the wire onto the back of the metal shape, allowing only a 1/4-inch (6 mm) length beyond the shape at one end, and the remaining length at the other end of shape (see figure 1).

6. Solder the wire to the back of the metal shape.

7. String a pearl onto the short end of the wire. Using a hammer, spread metal slightly at bottom to hold pearl. Snip off any excess if needed.

8. Form the longer end of the wire into a shepherd's hook for the ear wire.

9. Add patina using liver of sulfur. Polish lightly by hand.

PATTERN

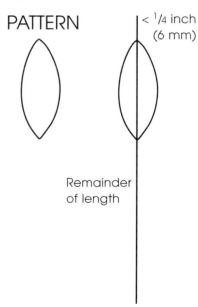

< 1/4 inch (6 mm)

Remainder of length

79

Pierced Spiral Pendant

Pierce a simple silver disk with a spiral design to create a simple, yet unique, pendant. You could use the same design to make lovely matching earrings.

You will need

- Silver sheet metal, 16-gauge
- Silver jump ring (or make your own from 20-gauge wire)
- Disk cutter
- Hammer
- Scribe
- Machinist's square
- Center punch
- Drill and small bit
- Bench pin or board for drilling surface
- Jeweler's saw and blade
- Steel block
- Dapping block and punches
- Buffing machine, buffing wheels, polishing compound

Here's How

Please see the *Tools & Supplies* chapter on how to cut a disk shape with disk cutters. Also see the *Techniques* chapter for detailed information on piercing metal.

Photo 1

Photo 2

Cut the Disk

1. Use a disk cutter to cut out a 1-inch (25 mm) disk from the silver sheet metal (see photo 1).

Pierce the Metal

2. Use a machinist's square to measure and find the center point of the disk. Scribe to mark for a center hole (see photo 2).

3. Use the center punch and a hammer to mark the hole in the center of the metal piece (see photo 3).

4. Lubricate the drill bit with beeswax before you begin drilling (see photo 4).

5. Using the drill, make a hole into the center of disk where it has been indented with the center punch. Use the bench pin as a surface for your drilling (see photo 5).

6. Insert a saw blade into one end of the saw frame. Thread the other end through the hole in the metal. Move the metal to be cut towards the end of the saw where the blade is fixed. Tighten the saw blade with the metal piece in place (see photo 6).

7. Place the metal piece on the bench pin. Begin sawing at the center hole, moving the saw blade up and down vertically while keeping the blade perfectly perpendicular (see photo 7).

8. Slowly move the saw blade around in a spiral as you saw up and down to create the design (see photo 8).

Finish

9. Drill a hole in the top center edge of the disk where a jump ring will be added.

10. Place the disk into the dapping block of a larger diameter and use the equivalent dapping punch to shape the metal into a concave form

11. Polish if desired.

12. Add the jump ring into the top hole and string onto a necklace chain.

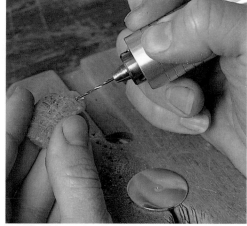
Photo 3

Photo 4

Photo 5

Photo 6

Photo 7

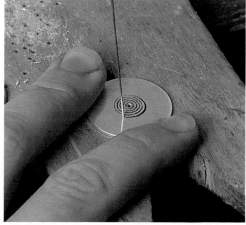
Photo 8

Gingko Earrings

I love to give my work interesting surface textures. One of my favorite tools to use to accomplish this is the cross peen hammer. This hammered finish gives these gingko earrings their distinctive quality. The hammer makes facets in the metal surface that catch and reflect the light, giving them a wonderful sparkle.

You will need

- 20 gauge sterling silver metal sheet
- Tracing paper, cardstock, pencil, scissors
- Scribe
- Jeweler's saw with 2/0 blade
- Bench pin
- Needle files, from medium to fine
- Ring clamp
- Steel block
- Cross peen hammer
- Flat-nose pliers
- Leather scrap
- Buffing machine, buffing wheel, polishing compound
- Center punch
- Drill and fine drill bit
- Ear wire finding

Here's How

Please see the *Techniques* chapter for detailed information on transferring designs, cutting the metal, and forging.

Create Earring Design

1. A pattern for the earring design is provided. Transfer this pattern onto cardstock and cut out. Place the pattern onto the sheet metal and trace around it with a scribe, marking the metal for sawing (see photo 1). Repeat for two shapes.

Cut and Refine the Piece

2. Place the metal on the bench pin. Cut out the two earring shapes using the jeweler's saw (see photo 2). Cut in an up and down motion, keeping saw perpendicular to surface (see photo 3).

3. Place one metal piece in a ring clamp so you can hold it without slipping or injuring your fingers. File away any sharp edges with needle files, working down from medium grade to a fine file (see photo 4, on page 84).

Pattern for Gingko Leaf

Photo 1

Photo 2

Photo 3

TIP

Plan your jewelry design before you begin. Use a mechanical pencil or ink and draw out designs on paper. Use a metal ruler for straight lines if they are intended to be straight. Think about connections and how pieces will join together.

Gingko Earrings

Texture

4. Place the cut out metal on a steel block. Use a cross peen hammer to texture the earring. Place the hammer's surface on the metal so the marks are vertical. Begin at the center of the leaf to hammer out towards each edge, rotating the leaf ever so slightly to account for the narrower top and wider bottom shape of the leaf (see photo 5). Allow the hammer marks to overlap.

5. Cut a piece of leather that fits into the jaws of your flat-nose pliers. This will prevent the pliers from making marks on the metal.

6. Use the cushioned pliers to bend the metal slightly in the center to create a crease. Then bend at each side of the center point to give the leaf form (see photo 6).

7. Repeat steps 4 through 6 to create the second earring shape.

Photo 4

Photo 5

Photo 6

TIP
Practice with your tools to make sure you are comfortable with how they work. Practice with the cross peen hammer on scraps of metal until you are able to make a consistent and pleasing pattern with it.

Finish

8. Buff the earring shapes lightly on the polishing wheel with polishing compound until they shine.

9. Use a center punch to indent the pieces at the top point of the shapes for the placement of the ear wires (see photo 7).

10. Drill a small hole at the indentation on each piece (see photo 8).

11. Add an ear wire to each earring shape (see photo 9).

12. Enjoy your finished earrings!

Photo 7

Photo 8

Photo 9

TIP

Ear wires can be purchased already made. However, it is easy to make your own ear wires from 20 or 22 gauge silver wire. On the end of the ear wire that will hold the earring in place, use a torch to melt the end, creating a bead on the end to act as a stop. Bend wire into a shepherd's hook.

Gingko Leaf Brooch

This Gingko Leaf Brooch looks great with the Gingko Earrings. The brooch design uses many of the same techniques as the Gingko Earrings, but there are also a few new ones for you to add to your list of skills.

You will need

- 18-gauge sterling silver sheet metal
- 10-gauge sterling silver round wire
- Tracing paper, cardstock, pencil, scissors
- Scribe
- Jeweler's saw
- Needle files
- Wire snips
- Flat-faced hammer
- Cross peen hammer
- Texture hammer
- Steel block
- Soldering supplies, medium solder
- Pickle & pickle pot
- Emery paper
- Pliers
- Hinged pin stem and clasp
- Buffing machine, buffing wheel, and polishing compound

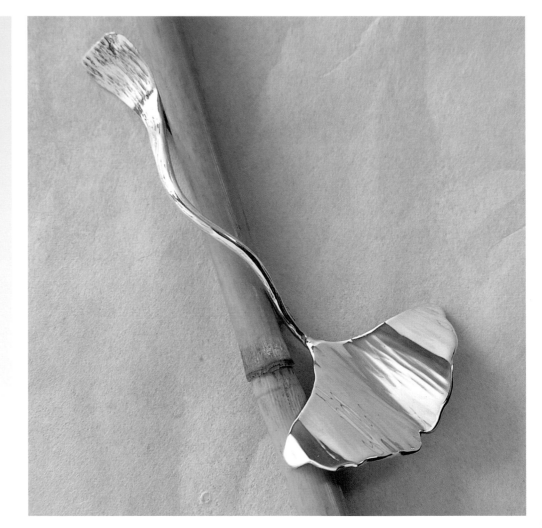

Pattern for Gingko Leaf

Here's How

Please see the *Tools & Supplies* and *Techniques* chapters for detailed information on transferring designs, cutting the metal, and forging.

Create the Leaf Design

1. A pattern for the brooch design is provided. Transfer this pattern onto cardstock and cut out. Place the pattern onto the sheet metal and trace around it with a scribe, marking the metal for sawing.

2. Saw gingko leaf shape out of the 18-gauge sterling using a jeweler's saw.

3. File the edges until smooth.

Fashion the Stem

4. Cut a 3-inch (76 mm) piece of 10-gauge round sterling wire using wire cutters (see photo 1).

5. Working on a steel block, forge a ¹/₂-inch (13 mm) area at both ends of the wire using a flat-faced hammer to slightly flatten out the ends of the wire (see photo 2). Both ends of the wire should be about one half of their original thickness and about twice their original width.

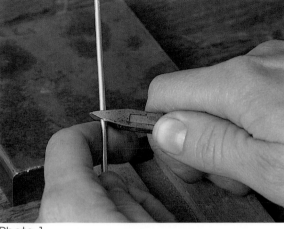
Photo 1

Photo 2

6. Continue to forge just one end of the wire, switching to a cross peen hammer. Keep the hammer parallel with the length of the wire, forging out one end into a fan shape (see photo 3). This will be the wide end of the stem that is opposite from the end that will be attached to the leaf. (Also refer to photo 4 to see the progression of the wire forging for the stem.)

Photo 3

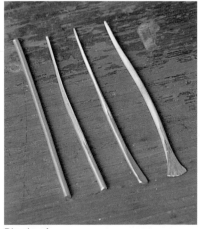
Photo 4

Gingko Leaf Brooch

Attach Stem

7. Solder the narrow end of the wire onto the point of the gingko leaf (on back) using medium solder (see photo 5).

8. Allow to air cool. Plunge into pickle solution (see photo 6). Let dry thoroughly.

9. Once the stem is attached, hammer very lightly to ease the transition from the sheet metal to the wire (leaf to stem).

10. Smooth this soldered area with needle files and emery paper until a natural progression from leaf to stem is achieved.

11. Hammer the leaf with a cross peen hammer to add texture to the leaf. Use the same technique for texturing the leaf as instructed in the Gingko Earrings.

12. Use a texture hammer to add additional interest to the stem (see photo 7).

Finish

13. Using pliers, bend the stem as desired to give it a natural curve.

14. Solder the pin stem hinge and clasp onto the back of brooch using easy solder. Pickle.

Photo 5

Photo 6

Photo 7

15. Polish your piece with the technique of your choice.

TIP

I make my own jeweler's hammers with textured heads. When these are used to strike the metal, they impart the same texture to the metal. Shown here is a texture hammer used to give the stem additional texture.

88

Gingko Pendant

Use the gingko leaf theme in miniature to create an elegant pendant. A frame box with an oxidized backing sets off the tiny gold gingko leaves that are cut from gold sheet metal and soldered to the backing.

You will need

- Silver wire, 2 mm square
- 20-gauge sterling silver sheet
- 22-gauge 18 karat yellow gold sheet
- 3 mm round silver tubing
- Tracing paper, cardstock, pencil, scissors
- Scribe
- Jeweler's saw with 8/0 blade
- Filing block
- Half-round file
- Soldering supplies, hard solder, medium, and easy solder
- Chasing tool with a straight line design
- Liver of sulfur
- Mixing bowl
- Tweezers
- Buffing machine, buffing wheel, and polishing compound
- Polishing cloth

Pattern

Continued on next page

Gingko Pendant

Here's How

Please see the *Tools & Supplies* and *Techniques* chapters for detailed information on transferring designs, cutting the metal, stamping, soldering, and oxidizing.

Create Frame

1. Create a frame box using the 2 mm square wire. Cut two top pieces of the frame, each measuring $7/8$ inch (22 mm) long. Cut two side pieces of the frame, each measuring 1 inch (25 mm) long.

2. File ends of each wire piece to a 45° angle. Use a filing block to ensure accurate angles (see photo 1).

3. Fit a top piece and a side piece together. Ensure that these form a 90° angle. Adjust by filing if necessary. Using hard solder, connect the top piece and the side piece of the frame (see photo 2). Repeat with the other two pieces to create two corners of the frame. Pickle.

4. Connect the last two corners with hard solder to form a perfect rectangle (see photo 3).

5. Stamp parallel lines around frame using the chasing tool (see photo 4).

6. Cut a piece from 20-gauge sterling sheet metal for the frame backing that measures $11/16$ x $13/16$ inch (17 x 21 mm). Measure the inside

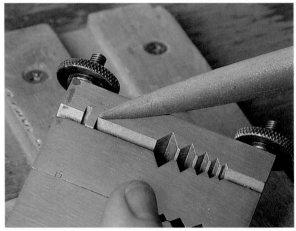
Photo 1

Photo 2

Photo 3

measurements of the frame before cutting to make sure you are cutting the correct size piece. Fit the backing into the frame and adjust size by filing if necessary.

7. Solder the rectangle to the inside of the frame using medium solder (see photo 5). Pickle.

Make Gingko Leaves

8. Transfer the gingko leaf pattern to cardstock and cut out. Place the pattern onto the yellow gold sheet and trace around it with a scribe.

9. Using a jeweler's saw and 8/0 blades, cut out the gingko leaves from the 22-gauge 18 karat yellow gold. The 8/0 blades will allow for extreme detail.

10. Stamp a design of radiating straight lines in the leaves using the chasing tool.

Finish

11. Solder onto back of leaves and solder leaves onto frame using easy solder.

12. Cut and solder a piece of 3 mm round tubing for a bail onto top of pendant. Pickle.

13. Polish and clean piece.

14. Add patina to the pendant with a liver of sulfur solution. Mix the solution in a bowl and drop piece into solution. Allow to remain in bowl until it turns dark gray

Photo 4

Photo 5

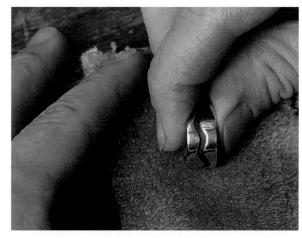

or black. Remove from bowl with tweezers. Rinse. Allow to dry.

15. Polish again to remove unwanted oxidation and to create a shine. Finish with a polishing cloth.

TIP

After adding patina to your piece, finish the polishing procedure by rubbing with a jewelry cloth. The photo on the left shows polishing a ring that has been oxidized with liver of sulfur. Keep a jewelry cloth handy and polish jewelry frequently to keep it shining.

Polished Anticlastic Bracelet

An anticlastic form is one that bends in two opposing directions at the same time. In this case, the metal curves to form the shape of the bracelet that bends around the wrist, and at the same time it bends upward from the center towards the edge. This anticlastic shape, along with the hammering, gives the bracelet a strength and springiness to retain its shape forever. The high polish on this bracelet is irresistible.

You will need
- 18-gauge sterling silver sheet metal
- Card stock to make pattern
- Jeweler's saw & sawblades
- Files
- Emery paper
- Vise
- Rawhide mallet
- Bracelet mandrel
- Nylon cross peen hammer
- Nylon stake for forming
- Planishing hammer
- Steel block
- Buffing machine, buffing wheel, and polishing compound

Pre-made Bracelet Blanks
Pre-cut bracelet blanks are also available. They are ready to be shaped and a pattern added to them if desired. Most bracelets blanks are between 5¹/₂ inches (14 cm) and 6¹/₂ inches (16.5 cm) in length, and from ¹/₂ inch (13 mm) to 3 inches (76 mm) in width. The space between the ends of the bracelet will vary depending on the size of the wearer's wrist, and in general is anywhere from ³/₄ inch (19 mm) to 1¹/₂ inches (38 mm).

Here's How

Please see the *Tools & Supplies* and *Techniques* chapters for detailed information on transferring designs, cutting the metal, forging, and polishing.

Cut the Metal

1. Make a pattern from card-stock for the bracelet shape. The one shown is ⁵/₈ inch (16 mm) wide and has tapered and rounded ends (see photo 1). Determine the bracelet length based on your wrist size, allowing enough room for the bracelet to be taken on and off comfortably. Allow a minimum of ¹/₂ inch (13 mm) between the ends of the bracelet.

2. Place the pattern onto the sheet metal. Using a scribe, trace around the pattern to mark the metal for cutting (see photo 2).

3. Cut the metal to the pattern shape using a jeweler's saw.

4. File the edge of the bracelet until it is perfectly smooth. A ring vise is used to hold the metal bracelet piece while filing (see photo 3).

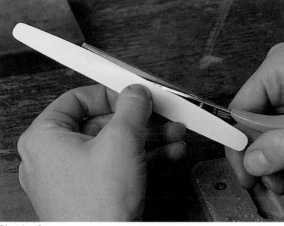
Photo 1

Photo 2

Photo 3

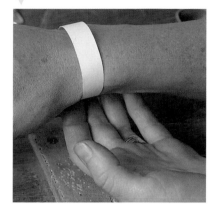

TIP
Try on the bracelet while you work and make adjustments as necessary.

Alternate Method

Use a glue stick to paste the paper design onto the metal, and then saw around the pattern as shown.

Polished Anticlastic Cuff Bracelet

Shape the Bracelet

5. Determine the circumference for your bracelet and mark that on the bracelet mandrel. Place the bracelet mandrel into a vise to hold it steady while forming the bracelet. Form the metal over the bracelet mandrel by striking metal with a rawhide mallet (see photo 4).

6. To create the concave shape, place the bracelet in a nylon stake with cutout forms. Use a nylon cross peen hammer to strike the center of the metal to shape it (see photo 5).

7. Place the bracelet on edge on a steel block. Using a planishing hammer, upset the edge of the bracelet by striking lightly on the edge (see photo 6). Try to draw the hammer and the metal from the inside of the bracelet outward, rotating the work as you go. Turn the bracelet over and repeat. Continue this process until the bracelet is curved to your liking.

8. Polish the bracelet to a high shine.

Photo 4

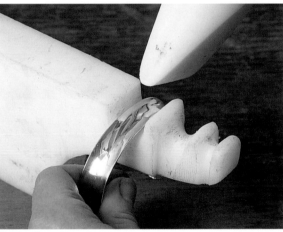

Photo 5

Photo 6

TIP

Keep the bracelet as symmetrical as possible. If using a tapered mandrel, turn the bracelet continually so the finished bracelet is not tapered.

This classic bracelet shape can take on many different looks depending on the finish. Here the surface of the bracelet has been hammered with the ball peen hammer before shaping the edge. The textured hammer marks catch the light and create interesting reflections. This bracelet was created using the same procedure as the Polished Anticlastic Cuff Bracelet, but it was cut to a 2-inch (50 mm) width.

This lovely bracelet with the abstract gold shapes was made using the same procedure as the Polished Anticlastic Cuff Bracelet. Before the last polishing step, gold shapes were cut from 26-gauge 18-karat gold sheet metal. These shapes were soldered onto the bracelet face. After pickling, the bracelet was polished.

Stamped Rings

The designs on these rings were created with chasing or stamping tools that create an impression in the metal. They are easily fabricated using the same methods for cutting, forming, and finishing the ring as instructed in the *River Rings* lesson. Instead of creating a die for the design and impressing it into the metal with a press, the chasing tools and stamps are simply struck with a hammer to impress each design.

You will need

- 14-gauge or 1.5 mm sheet metal (this is the minimum thickness)
- Ring-sizing gauge
- Chasing tools
- Steel block
- Hammer
- Ring vise
- Files
- Emery paper
- Ring mandrel
- Rawhide mallet
- Bench vise
- Ring-bending pliers (with one half-round jaw and one square jaw)
- Soldering supplies using medium or hard solder
- Liver of sulfur and fine brush for applying
- Flexible shaft machine with abrasive wheel
- Buffing machine, buffing wheel, and polishing compound
- Polishing cloth

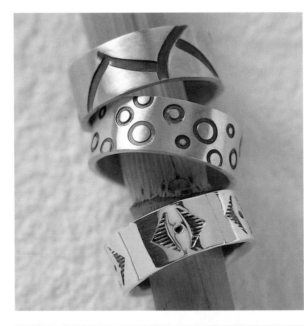

Here's How

Please see the *Tools & Supplies* and *Techniques* chapters for detailed information on transferring designs, cutting the metal, forming, stamping, oxidizing, and polishing.

Cut the Metal

1. Measure finger size using the ring-sizing gauge.

2. Cut material to length needed for ring (see photo 1).

3. Anneal the metal if needed to make it malleable.

Stamp the Design

4. Place the metal on a steel block. Hold the stamp of your choice against the metal piece using your thumb and forefinger. Anchor your hand and wrist on the metal block and any surrounding table or bench. Rock the stamp back and forth slightly to make certain that it is flat on the surface of the metal. Stamp the design into the metal by striking the stamp with the hammer (see photo 2). Hit the stamp squarely and solidly. Attempt to do this only once as repeated stamping often creates shadows. Keep the stamping strong, but not so deep so as to shear the metal.

5. Anneal again if needed so that the metal can be rounded to a ring shape. Stamping is a form of work-hardening the metal so it may need to be made malleable again after the stamping is complete.

Form the Ring

6. Determine the ring size on the ring mandrel and mark. Anchor the mandrel in a vise. Place the metal piece on the mark of the mandrel. Form the piece into a ring shape by striking with the rawhide mallet.

7. Bring the ends of the ring together with the aid of the ring-bending pliers. It does not matter at this point if the ring is round. A *D* shape is preferable as the ends can meet flush on the flat side of the *D*. Bring the ends together for a perfect fit. If there is any gap at all, file until a perfect fit is achieved. No light should be visible through the seam.

8. Solder seam using medium or hard solder. Quench in water to cool. Pickle. Dry thoroughly.

9. Place the ring on the ring mandrel again and use a rawhide mallet to gently round out and refine the ring. Pull the ring off the ring mandrel and turn it 180°. Place it back onto the mandrel. Continue hammering until desired size is achieved.

Finish

10. Sand and polish as needed.

11. Add patina if desired to highlight stamping.

12. Polish with a polishing cloth to remove excess patina.

Stamping tools showing designs on ends.

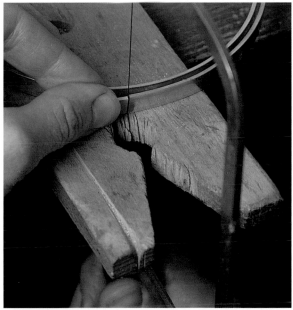
Photo 1

Photo 2

TIPS

• If you are stamping letters onto the metal you will want to be careful of the alignment of the letters. For very precise alignment, use a piece of tape as a guide for the bottom edge of the stamp. Check spacing and placement of stamps by looking at the reflection of the stamp in the metal as it is near the surface of the metal.

• Practice stamping on scrap pieces of metal with different weight hammers until satisfactory results are achieved. You will want to get the force of the strike just right so that the impression is deep enough to show, but not so deep that it pressed through the metal. Also, you will need practice in holding the stamp exactly perpendicular to the surface so that the impression is even.

• For stamped rings, choose a flat wire that is a minimum of 14-gauge or sheet metal of a 1.5 mm thickness. Using metal any thinner than this will not give a good impression when stamped.

River Rings

Rings are simple to make and fun to wear. Once the basic shape of your ring has been made, add stamped designs, create hammered textures, or solder multiple wires together to create interesting patterns.

The rings shown here have been impressed with a wavy line that represents a river. This was accomplished by impressing a steel wire shape (or die) into the metal with a hydraulic press. You can create a similar look by stamping designs into the ring with chasing tools as illustrated in the *Stamped Rings* project following this.

You will need

- Flat sterling silver wire, 8 mm x 1.5 mm
- Steel wire (to make die or ready made steel die)
- Ring-sizing gauge
- Round-nose pliers, 2 pairs
- Steel blocks, 2
- Hydraulic press
- Ring vise
- Files
- Emery paper
- Ring mandrel
- Rawhide mallet
- Bench vise
- Ring-bending pliers (with one half-round jaw and one square jaw)
- Soldering supplies using medium or hard solder
- Liver of sulfur and fine brush for applying
- Flexible shaft machine with abrasive wheel
- Buffing machine, buffing wheel, and polishing compound
- Polishing cloth

A single river line was impressed into this ring. The river line in this ring has been oxidized with liver of sulfur to create a stunning two-toned ring.

These rings have been impressed with double river lines. The same die was used for each line, but it was positioned differently. Also, no patina was added to the river lines.

Here's How

Please see the *Tools & Supplies* and *Techniques* chapters for detailed information on transferring ring designs, cutting the metal, forming, using a hydraylic press, oxidizing, and polishing.

Cut the Metal

1. Determine the size of your ring by trying on rings from ring sizer until you find the right fit (see photo 1). This will help you determine the length of metal material needed for the ring.

2. Using a jeweler's saw, cut the length needed of the flat sterling silver wire (see photo 2).

Impress the Design

3. To create a die for the wavy design on ring, use two pairs of round-nose pliers to form the steel wire (see photo 3).

4. Place the steel wire on the flat sterling silver material, taking care to note the position of the steel wire at the ends of the silver. The wire needs to be placed in the same position on both ends so that when the ring ends are soldered together, the design lines match up for a seamless looking ring. Tape the steel wire and silver down to a steel block to prevent unwanted movement (see photo 4).

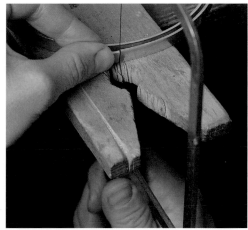
Photo 1

Photo 2

Photo 3

Photo 4

Photo 5

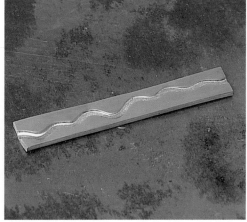
Photo 6

99

River Rings

5. Place the steel block with the metal taped to it into in a hydraulic press. Place another steel block over the steel/silver sandwich (see photo 5 on page 97).

6. Crank the hydraulic cylinder using moderate force to press the steel into the silver. Release the pressure and check impression. Remember, it is always easy to do more, but over-doing it means redoing it from the beginning. Remove metal from press and lift off the die to reveal the impressed silver metal (see photo 6 on page 97).

Form the Ring

7. Hold ring in a ring vise and use a file to create perfectly square straight ends on the silver piece (see photo 7).

8. Mark your ring size on the ring mandrel. Anchor the ring mandrel in a vise. Place the metal ring piece at that mark on the mandrel. Form the metal into a ring shape by striking it with a rawhide mallet (see photo 8).

9. Use ring-bending pliers to help bring the ends together for a perfect fit (see photo 9).

10. Solder the seam of the ring using medium or hard solder (see photo 10). Quench in water to cool. Pickle. Let dry thoroughly.

Photo 7

Photo 8

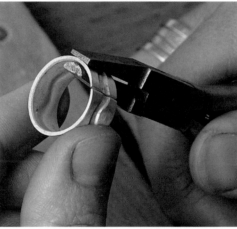

Photo 9

TIP

At the stage at which the soldering is done, it does not matter if the ring is round. A *D* shape is preferable as the ends can meet flush on the flat side of the *D*. If there is any gap at all, file or saw until a perfect fit is achieved. No light should be visible through the seam.

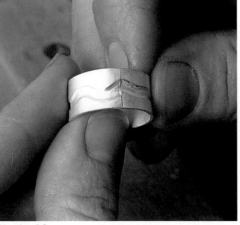

Photo 10

Photo 11

11. Place your ring on the ring mandrel and strike with a rawhide mallet to gently round out and refine the ring shape (see photo 11). Pay attention to the size markings on the mandrel when placing your ring. It is very easy to stretch a ring to a much larger size than desired. Pull the ring off the ring mandrel, turn it 180°, and place it back on the mandrel. Continue hammering until desired size is achieved.

Finish

12. File the seam, inside and outside, with a fine file (see photo 12).

13. Clean up and smooth the outside and inside of the ring with emery paper (see photo 13).

14. Finish cleaning up the rough places on the ring using an abrasive wheel in the flex shaft (see photo 14).

15. Polish the ring with a buffing wheel (see photo 15).

16. Using liver of sulfur and a fine brush, add patina to the impressed area of the ring (see photo 16).

17. Finish by polishing ring with a polishing cloth to remove any excess patina (see photo 17).

Photo 12

Photo 13

Photo 14

Photo 15

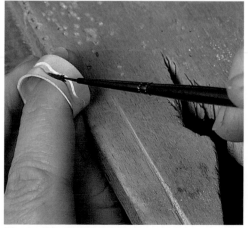

Photo 16

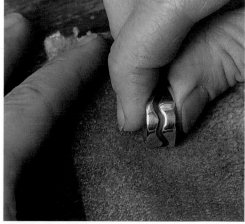

Photo 17

Ring Variations

Rocky River Rings

These sterling silver rings have the same river impressions as the *River Rings* project. To make this ring design, follow the *River Rings* instructions from step one through step six. After you have made the river impression, roll the sterling silver through the rolling mill with a coarse piece of emery paper. Follow steps 7 through 17 to complete the rings. Liver of sulfur was painted onto the entire ring to emphasize the pebbly texture as well as the river line.

Golden Ring

This ring has been fabricated in 18 karat yellow gold. The ring was textured by striking it with a cross-peen hammer. The ring was constructed using the same procedure as for the *Stamped Rings*. Instead of stamping a design into the metal as instructed in step 4, the metal was textured with a cross peen hammer at this stage. Here is a quick recap of how to construct this ring: cut the metal strip, texture it with the cross peen hammer, shape it to the ring form, solder the joint, smooth the seam, and then polish.

Leaf Prints Collection

As much as we all try to imitate nature, few designs can compare to the beauty and detail of naturally occurring elements. To make this collection of jewelry pieces, use actual leaves to impress the metal, capturing the immense detail and texture of the foliage. Dry the leaves or natural materials thoroughly before attempting to use them in the rolling mill. Place the leaves atop the metal piece and then roll the sandwich through a rolling mill. This process captures the beauty of nature.

You will need

- Metal of your choice, silver shown
- Dried leaf
- Rolling mill
- Soldering torch
- Metal snips
- Jeweler's saw
- Ring vise
- Files
- Round-nose pliers
- Polishing supplies
- Liver of sulfur and fine brush
- Soldering supplies, easy solder
- Polishing cloth

A small fern leaf was used to impress the veining as well as a guide for the actual shape of this pendant. To make this pendant, choose a fern leaf for your design impression and dry it thoroughly. Excess moisture will result in a poor imprint on the metal. Cut a piece of metal slightly larger than the fern leaf. It is important to leave a little extra metal for the slight expansion of the leaf as it goes through the rolls of the rolling mill. If you can't find a fern leaf the size you desire, simply draw a pattern of the cutout shape you want. Place the fern leaf on the metal strip and roll through the rolling mill. After impressing the design on the metal, use the pattern to cut the metal to the shape you wish.

Pictured is a leaf print pendant. See the following pages for other leaf imprinted pieces in this collection.

Leaf Prints Collection

Here's How

Please see the *Tools & Supplies* and *Techniques* chapters for detailed information on using the rolling mill, cutting the metal, forming, and polishing.

Texture the Metal

1. Cut a piece of metal to the approximate size needed for the jewelry piece you are making. To prepare the metal, anneal it so that it is soft and malleable or order it directly from the supplier dead soft. Polish to remove all scratches and fire scale.

2. Place the dried leaf on top of the metal piece, with the textured side facing the metal. Insert the set into the rolling mill with widest part of the leaf to go through the rolls first (see photo 1).

3. Roll from start to finish without stopping (see photo 2). When the metal clears the mill it is ready to be fabricated into the piece of jewelry. Wipe the rolls down and oil them after use to prevent rust.

Cut & Shape the Metal

4. Use metal snips to cut and trim the metal roughly around the shape of the leaf (see photo 3).

Photo 1

Photo 2

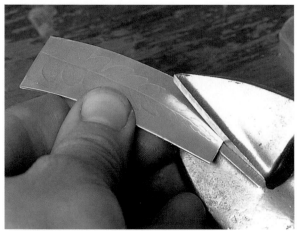

Photo 3

Finding Leaves

Because leaves are so delicate, it is a process of trial and error to find leaves that will stand up to the immense pressure of the rolling mill and will imprint well into metal. Sturdy ferns work well as do leaves with heavy veining and texture. Drying the leaves thoroughly by placing in a flat leaf press or a book is the first step. Test the leaf using the rolling mill with a scrap of metal. Experiment with the rolls and pressure to get a satisfactory imprint. Too little pressure will leave a shallow imprint. Too much pressure will distort the leaf and metal.

TIP

It is important to keep rolling until the metal has gone completely through the mill. If the action of the rolling is interrupted or ceases, often times the leaf will break or leave a bump in the finished work at this point. This piece shows a good impression of the leaf on the metal.

5. Saw the outside edge of the pendant piece to give it the same edge detail as the leaf itself (see photo 4). Cut a long leaf stem so that it can be used to create a bail for the pendant. When making earrings, cut the metal just at the top of the leaf, allowing no extra stem.

6. Place the metal piece in a ring vise to hold it securely. Use files to refine the edge of the piece (see photo 5).

Finish

7. Use round-nose pliers to bend the extra stem piece around to the back of the leaf to create a bale (see photo 6).

8. Using easy solder, attach the end of the bale to the back of the pendant. Cool and pickle.

9. Polish carefully by hand so that you don't remove the leaf impression.

10. Add patina to accentuate the leaf texture. Polish away excess patina with a polishing cloth.

Photo 4

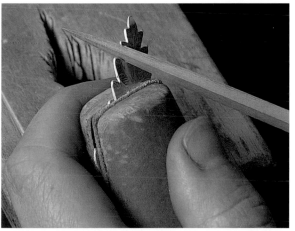
Photo 5

Photo 6

TIP

If findings are needed on pieces such as earrings, solder findings to the work using as little heat and solder as necessary. The goal is to prevent fire scale and the need to polish. Excessive polishing on the polishing wheel can destroy the leaf imprint in seconds.

Leaf Prints Collection

This silver pendant and earring set are natural beauties. The disks for the earrings and pendants were cut from pieces of metal that were impressed with a natural leaf design by rolling through a mill. Cut your own disks with a circle cutter or purchase ready-cut disks from jewelry suppliers. Run them through the rolling mill with a dried leaf atop the metal to give them texture. After impressing the design, drill a small hole at the top of each piece to attach the findings. Use earring findings for the earrings and attach a jump ring to the pendant.

Make a simple yet beautiful ring by impressing the metal with a leaf. See *River Rings* project for details on constructing the ring shape. After cutting the flat wire metal for the ring piece, roll it through the rolling mill with a leaf on top to impress the design into it. Shape, solder, and then polish the ring to finish.

For earrings, create two mirror impressions by using the leaf sandwiched in between two pieces of metal when rolling through the rolling mill. Solder a small piece of wire to the end of the leaf to add a small fresh water pearl. At the end of the pearl, forge the wire to spread it slightly so that the pearl won't slip off the wire.

For larger pins or brooches, cut the metal into a geometric shape that frames the leaf and gives a good border to the work. Shown here is a beautiful brooch with a leaf impression in the center of the 1^1/$_2$-inch x 3-inch (38 x 76 mm) sterling silver rectangle. After impressing the leaf into the silver metal rectangle, form the piece over a bracelet mandrel, by hand to create the convex shape.

Hollow Beads Pendant & Earrings

These textured, hollow beads make interesting pendants and earrings, or can be strung together to make a bracelet or necklace.

You will need

- Metal of your choice
- Rolling mill
- Items to give the metal texture such as metal screening or textured hard plastic
- 20-gauge silver wire
- 2 pearls for pendant, each 6 mm
- 2 disk beads for pendant, each 8 mm
- 2 silver beads for pendant, each 3 mm
- 2 silver beads for earrings, each 3mm
- Disk cutters
- Files
- Dapping tools and block
- Hammer
- Leather scrap
- 320 grit emery paper
- Soldering supplies
- Buffing machine, buffing wheel, and polishing compound
- Liver of sulfur and fine brush

Here's How

Please see the *Tools & Supplies* and *Techniques* chapters for detailed information on using the rolling mill, cutting the metal, forming, oxidizing, and polishing.

Texture the Metal

1. Cut a piece of metal that is large enough to cut out two pendant pieces and four earring pieces. Each pendant piece measures 1¹/8 inch (28 mm) diameter. Each earring piece measures ³/4-inch (19 mm) diameter. To prepare the metal, anneal it so that it is soft and malleable or order it directly from the supplier dead soft. Polish to remove all scratches and fire scale.

2. Place the textured metal piece on top of the metal piece. Insert the set into the rolling mill. Roll from start to finish without stopping.

Cut the Metal

3. Using a disk cutter, punch out two circles of the textured metal in desired sizes (see photo 1) for each jewelry piece. For the pendants shown, the disks are 1¹/8 inches (28 mm) in diameter and the earrings are ³/4 inch (19 mm) in diameter.

4. File off burrs and make circles as perfect as possible.

Form Metal

5. Place disks with design side down into dapping block. Begin using a much larger depression than the circle, and hammer the properly sized dapping tool slowly. Too much hammering will obliterate the texture. Work in successively smaller sized hemispheres in the dapping block until desired shape is achieved (see photo 2). Remove domed metal from dapping block.

TIP

Protect a very delicate pattern by placing a circle of leather in the bottom of the dapping block.

6. Sand outside edge lightly on 320 grit emery paper to create a flat edge on each domed piece.

Create Hollow Beads

7. With a needle file, create two small grooves in the flat edge of each disk for placement of ear wire or wires for stringing beads (see photo 3). The impressions need to be exactly opposite one another on each disk.

8. Prepare to solder two domes together to make each bead. Make a depression in a firebrick to hold bead steadily in place while soldering. Flux lightly, allowing flux to dry

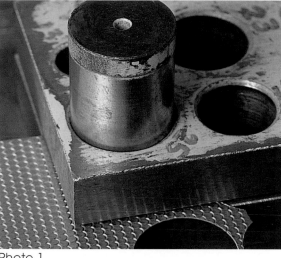
Photo 1

Photo 2

Photo 3

thoroughly before placing solder and dome on top. Match up the filed grooves on the sides. Place chips of solder just inside the flat edge. Heat lightly with torch around the edge of the bead. Attempt to draw the solder out toward the edge of the bead with the heat of the torch. Cool, pickle, and rinse.

Finish

9. Polish and patina if desired.

Making Pendant and Earrings

For earrings: Push wire through the domes where you made the impressions with the file. String a small silver bead on the end of the wire. Hammer the tip of the wire to keep bead securely in place. Shape the other end of the wire into ear hooks.

For pendant: Cut a wire piece 2³⁄₄ inches (70 mm) long. Twist an eye at the end of the wire piece. String a silver bead, a disk bead, and then the pearl onto the wire and push up to the eye. Push wire through the hollow metal disk where impressions were made. String a pearl, a disk, and a small silver bead on the other end of the wire. Hammer the tip of the wire to spread it so that the beads will stay securely in place.

Reticulated Pendants and Ring

A controlled melting called reticulation produces an abstract pattern on the surface of metal. It is never exactly the same twice. Here silver has been reticulated, then cut into disks to make a centerpiece for a pendant and a ring.

You will need

- Reticulation silver
- 10-gauge round silver wire
- 3 mm silver tubing
- Torch
- Firebrick
- Disk cutter
- Dapping tools and dapping block
- 320, 400, and 600 grit emery paper
- Mandrel
- Soldering supplies, easy, medium and hard solders
- Burnishing tool
- Files
- Buffing machine, buffing wheel, polishing compound
- Liver of sulfur
- Polishing cloth

An intriguing pendant and ring were fashioned from reticulated metal that was cut into disks, shaped into a convex dome, and bordered with silver wire. Findings were soldered to the back. The disk for the pendant was cut to 1¹/₄ inches (32 mm) in diameter, and the ring disk was cut to ³/₄ inch (19 mm) diameter.

Pendant on opposite page: The reticulated pendant was placed on a handmade sterling silver chain. There are fifteen ³/₄-inch (19 mm) silver circles that are linked with sixteen ³/₄-inch (19 mm) oval links. The circles are soldered with 10-gauge round wire links flattened with a planishing hammer on a steel block. The long ovals are shaped from 18-gauge silver wire. After forming into ovals, use them to link the circles together. Solder the seams of the ovals and polish.

Reticulated Pendants and Ring

Here's How

Read the information in the *Techniques* chapter for details on the reticulation process.

Texture the Metal

1. Reticulate a piece of silver using the instructions in the *Reticulation* lesson. (See photos 1 and 2 for the reticulation steps.)

Cut & Shape Disks

2. Punch out circles of desired reticulated metal using a disk cutter (see photo 3).

3. Form the disks into a dome by lightly tapping with a dapping tool in dapping block.

4. Sand edges of the disk flat with 320 grit emery paper.

5. Measure the outside circumference of the domed reticulated metal. Cut a piece of 10-gauge round silver wire to this size. Form the wire around a mandrel to the same circumference as the dome.

6. Solder the joint of the wire circle with hard solder. Quench then pickle.

Photo 1

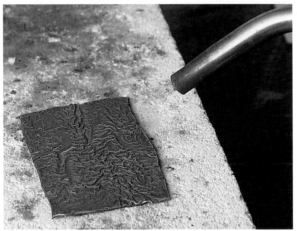
Photo 2

Photo 3

7. Before soldering the reticulated metal to the circle border, burnish edges with a burnishing tool as reticulated metal is porous and tends to absorb solder.

8. Lay the dome against the round wire border. Flux and then place chips of solder around perimeter. Solder with medium solder. Pickle and dry.

Finish

9. To make a pendant you will need to attach a finding for sliding it onto a necklace. Cut a 1/8-inch (3 mm) piece of 3 mm tubing. File the ends to smooth. Solder this piece of tubing with easy solder to the back side of the pendant. Pickle and dry.

10. To make a ring, solder a silver ring to the back of the reticulated dome. See information in the *River Rings* project for information on how to form a silver ring.

11. Use 400 to 600 emery paper to remove fire scale and excess solder from the jewelry piece. Polish as desired.

12. Add patina as desired with liver of sulfur. Remove excess patina by hand using a polishing cloth.

This beautiful little locket-sized pendant is fabricated from a piece of reticulated metal cut into a $^3/_4$ x $^7/_8$-inch (19 x 22 mm) rectangle. The piece was framed with 10-gauge square silver wire. See the *Gingko Pendant* project for information on how to make a frame around a piece. The finding for attaching to a necklace is soldered to the top of the frame. The finding was cut $^1/_8$ inch (3 mm) long from 5 mm silver tubing.

This pendant is very dramatic with its interesting pattern and the horizontal positioning of the pendant rectangle. To make this pendant, cut a piece of reticulated metal to 1$^1/_4$ inches x 1 inch (32 x 25 mm). Frame it with 10-gauge square silver wire. See the *Gingko Pendant* project for information on how to make a frame. Cut a $^3/_{16}$-inch (5 mm) piece of 3 mm silver tubing to create a finding for attaching the pendant to a necklace chain. Solder this tubing to the top of the frame.

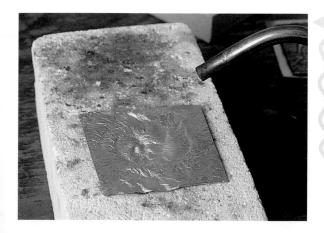

TIP
The metal will melt with different textures, depending upon how you move the torch around the metal. The torch was moved around the metal in a spiral fashion to create this texture.

Bezel Set Stone Pendant & Variations

A bezel is a thin metal wall that holds a stone in place. Bezels are most often used to hold cabochons, but can also be used for faceted stones instead of prong settings. Very thin metal is formed around the shape of the stone to frame the stone.

You will need

- 24-gauge silver bezel wire
- 16-gauge sterling silver round wire
- Ammonite stone, 8 mm x 10 mm
- Jeweler's saw frame and blade
- Burnishing tool
- Wooden dowel, 5/16 inch (8 mm) in diameter
- Pliers
- Emery paper
- Soldering supplies
- Flexible shaft machine and abrasive wheel

This beautiful ammonite cabochon stone is set in a silver bezel and enhanced with a fanned-out coil of sterling silver. A chain can be threaded through one of the rings of the coil so that it can be worn as a pendant.

Here's How

Please see the *Techniques* chapter for detailed information on bezel settings and soldering.

Cut Metal

1. Roll out the bezel wire. Measure the circumference of stone to determine length of wire needed. Form wire into the approximate shape of the stone using pliers (see photo 1).

2. Fit wire around stone and make adjustments. Cut wire to the length needed using a jeweler's saw. Cut down the height of the wire if needed. It should be tall enough to grasp the stone, but not so tall as to obscure it. When in doubt, make it taller, it can always be sanded down. Anneal the wire if it is too springy. Place the stone in a safe place to be positioned later.

Solder

3. Flux the joint of the wire and solder using medium or hard solder. Pickle. When in doubt,

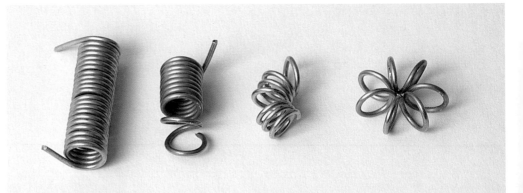

Stages of coil decoration

114

make the bezel wire ever so slightly too small and hammer it lightly to stretch if needed. A bezel that is too big will need to be cut apart and re-soldered. Place the bezel around the stone and test the fit. Adjust as needed.

4. Cut a piece of sheet metal for a backing for the bezel. Cut it slightly larger than the size of the bezel. Sand the bottom edge of the bezel to ensure that it is perfectly flat. Re-check the shape of bezel to stone, and test to make certain that the stone can be dropped in from above.

5. Flux and place the solder chips flat on the metal just touching the edge of the bezel. Solder the wire bezel to the backing. When possible, heat from underneath to help draw the solder around the edge of the bezel wire. Heating from above will often cause the thin bezel wire to heat prematurely and melt, or cause the solder to be drawn up onto the bezel wire. Air cool and pickle.

6. Cut the sheet metal backing around the bezel to the shape of the bezel using a jeweler's saw (see photo 2). File and sand to finish.

Form the Pendant

7. Wrap the 16-gauge silver wire around a rod or dowel to form more than seven coils. Snip off extra length so that you have exactly seven

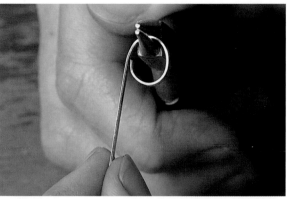
Photo 1

Photo 2

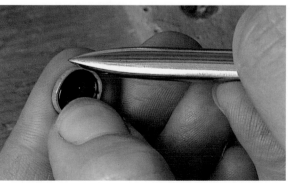
Photo 3

circles. Pull the coil around into a circle. (See photo on previous page for the stages of making the coil.)

8. Position and fit this coil onto the backside of the bezel unit. Solder the circles of the coil to one another at the center so that it is stationary. Solder the coil to the back-side of the bezel unit.

9. If you are going to make a jewelry piece other than a pendant that might need findings, attach the findings at this point before setting the stone.

10. Use a soft abrasive wheel on the flex shaft to polish out any scratches. Tiny buffs will help bring the work to shiny perfection.

11. Check the top edge of the bezel with the stone and sand if needed. Use a bur-nishing tool to slightly bend the bezel away from the edge to allow for fitting of the stone. Very gently and carefully fit the stone, never pushing it into place until you are certain that it is ready to be set. When the stone is in place, begin pushing the bezel wire over the stone, working slowly around the stone and continually check-ing the height of the bezel. Continue burnishing until the stone is securely set in place (see photo 3).

Bezel Set Stone Pendant & Variations

This silver ring features a 1/2 x 3/4 inch (12 x 18 mm) carnelian cabochon stone. The base for the bezel was cut slightly wider than the bezel setting. The edge of the bezel base was hammered with a cross peen hammer to give it texture. The ring is 1/4 inch (6 mm) wide and soldered to the back of the bezel base.

The stone in this sterling silver ring is ruby in zoisite. The stone measures 1 1/8 x 5/8 inches (28 x 16 mm) at the widest point. The ring section is 1/4 inch (6 mm) wide and was given a texture using the cross peen hammer before it was soldered to the back of the bezel setting.

The stone in this exquisite brooch is petrified dinosaur bone measuring 3/4 x 1 inch (18 x 25 mm) and set in a silver bezel. The top metal triangle on this piece is reticulated brass and silver. The brass is an 8-gauge piece while the silver is a 20-gauge piece. The two pieces were sweat soldered together. 18-gauge wire pieces are soldered on to connect the top triangle to the bezel set stone piece. A pin back finding is soldered to the back of the jewelry piece.

Pictured opposite: A combination of skills presented in this book were used to create this lovely necklace. The moss agate stone set in a bezel measures approximately 1 x 1 1/8 inches (25 x 28 mm). The backing was cut slightly larger than the setting to create a base with a border. Because agates are translucent and I wanted light coming through the stone, I made a cutout shape in the back of the base piece. Two smaller 3/4-inch (19 mm) triangles of reticulated and patinated silver were set in bezel. No base piece of metal was needed for these pieces. Six 8 mm silver pearls add elegance to the piece. The necklace gets its length from ten pieces of 1 inch (25 mm) long 12-gauge square silver wire that have been textured with a cross peen hammer. All the elements of this jewelry piece are connected with jump rings soldered to the metal pieces. Wire was threaded through the holes in the beads to connect them. A barrel clasp finding finishes the piece.

Bezel Set Stone Pendant & Variations

Turquoise, so popular today, is fabricated into a stunning silver pendant. The stone measures 32 mm x 48 mm and is set in a silver bezel with a base that is wider than the bezel set stone piece. The base is cut with a curved edge rather than straight to make it more interesting. Three tiny silver beads of 2 mm, 1½ mm, and 1 mm sizes are soldered to the base piece at each point of the triangle. Patina on the piece defines the beads nicely. A loop of 12-gauge silver wire is soldered to the back of the piece so that it could be strung on a necklace or chain.

This shows the back of the pendant piece. The base metal piece is pierced with a spiral design. This added a special personal finishing touch to the piece. For details on the piercing technique, see the *Piercing* lesson in the *Techniques* chapter. Notice the 12-gauge silver wire loop that is soldered to the back for stringing the necklace chain. It is a half-circle, with the flat cut ends soldered to the back, rather than a full circle loop.

Cast Pendant & Earrings

Cast textured disk shapes in pewter using the direct cast method to make intriguing earrings and pendant. Make a mold by carving the shapes into cuttlefish bone. Pour molten metal directly into the mold. Here simple shallow dome-shaped disks were carved into the bone for the pendant, measuring 1^1/$_4$ inches (31 mm) diameter, and the earrings, measuring ^{3}/$_4$ inch (18 mm) diameter.

You will need

- Cuttlefish bone (large ones can be cut in half)
- Jeweler's saw
- Sandpaper (100-200 grit for sanding cuttlefish flat on one side)
- Carving tools (for clay) or dental tools
- Small paintbrush
- Duct tape or steel binding wire
- Coffee can
- Crucible (different one for each metal you use)
- Charcoal block or firebrick
- Metal for casting, pewter is preferred
- Water for cooling castings
- Drill with fine bit
- Ear wire findings
- 4 mm silver tubing

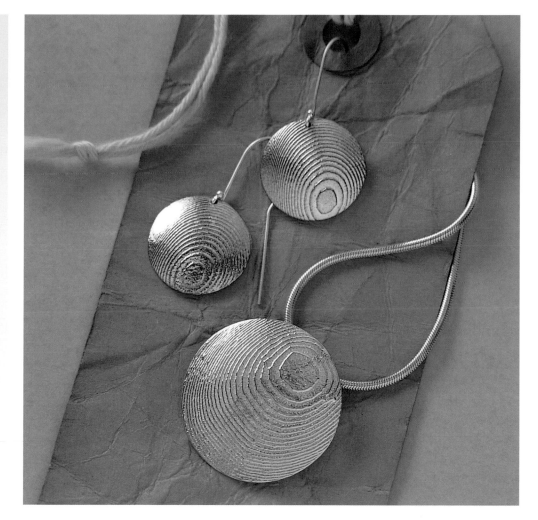

CAUTION

Contamination warning: Keep tools used for pewter separate from other tools. Small bits of pewter can contaminate silver and other metals, so keep a set of tools and preferably a work area separate for pewter work.

Cast Pendant & Earrings

Here's How

Please see the *Techniques* Chapter for detailed information on direct casting.

Creating the Mold

1. Prepare the cuttlefish bone by removing both ends with a saw or sawing in half if the cuttlefish bone is very large. With the soft side down, rub on sandpaper to create a flat surface on the cuttlefish bone (see photo 1).

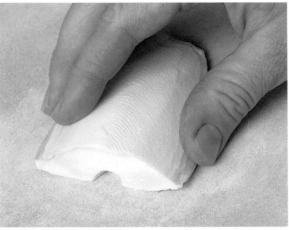
Photo 1

2. Use a carving tool or scribe to create a funnel in one end of the bone (see photo 2). This will be the opening for pouring in the molten metal.

3. At the bottom of this funnel, begin carving a design of your choice. Here a shallow domed circle has been carved for the pendant shape (see photo 3 for carving progression). To make molds for the earrings carve two domes, each ³/₄ inch (19 mm) in diameter. For the pendant as pictured, carve a dome 1¹/₄ inches (31 mm) in diameter. As you carve, use a small brush to remove all bits of dust from the cavity. This will help expose the grain in the cuttlefish.

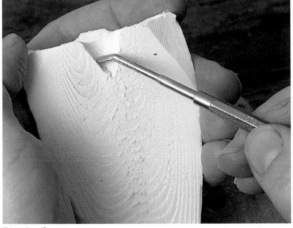
Photo 2

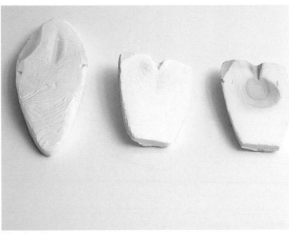
Photo 3

TIP

In general, keep designs within ¹/₂ inch (13 mm) from the perimeter of the bone. Do not carve too deeply, and make designs trail downward from the funnel. Think of the metal as it is poured into the funnel and flows down through the design in the cuttlefish. Molten metal does not like to travel upwards.

120

4. Press the cuttlefish bone against a charcoal block, a firebrick, or piece of plaster. The design will be encased. Hold this up to the light and look to see if any cracks are visible. Use wire or duct tape to secure the two together (see photo 4). Duct tape is sufficient for low temperature melting metals such as pewter. For silver and brass, use steel binding wire.

Pouring the Metal

5. Place cuttlefish bone in a coffee can or metal tray. This will be the surface where the mold will rest while pouring. Use non-combustible materials to prop it up so that it won't tip or fall over.

6. Heat pewter with a torch in a cast iron crucible from underneath (see photo 5). Extinguish flame.

7. Immediately pour the metal slowly and carefully into the cuttlefish mold (see photo 6).

Photo 4

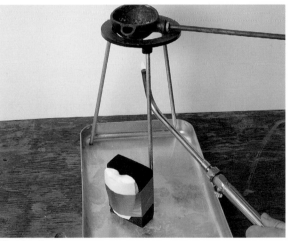
Photo 5

Photo 6

TIP
Molten metal will find the tiniest crevice to escape, so if any light can be seen, sand the cuttlefish lightly to make the surface absolutely flat.

Cast Pendant & Earrings

8. Allow to cool for three to five minutes. Remove tape or wire carefully (see photo 7).

9. Use tweezers to remove casting from cuttlefish mold (see photo 8). Careful extraction can allow for multiple castings from one mold.

10. Quench metal in a cup of cool water.

11. Using a jeweler's saw, cut off the cast area of the funnel (see photo 9).

Finish

12. To make the pendant, solder a 1/8-inch (3 mm) piece of tubing onto the back of the pendant piece. For the earrings, drill a small hole at the top of each cast piece.

13. File and polish as needed.

14. Add the ear wire findings to the earrings.

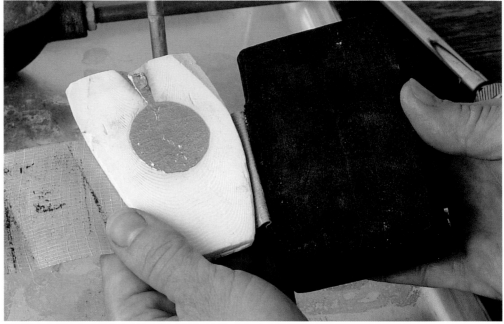
Photo 7

Photo 8

Photo 9

These pendants were created using the same method described for the pendant and earrings. Interesting shapes are easy to carve into cuttlefish bone. The teardrop shaped pendant on the left measures $^3/_4$ x 2 inches (18 x 51 mm). The pendant on the right has the same measurements, but the bone was carved deeper around the edges to create the interesting raised border.

Cast Leaf Belt Buckle

A real leaf was used to create the leaf pattern in this metal piece. Lost wax casting method was used to make the piece.

You will need

All of these supplies are especially made for the lost wax casting process. You can find them where jewelry-making supplies are sold.

- Wax carving tools
- Soft carving wax
- Denatured alcohol
- Sprue wax
- Spiral saw blades
- Alcohol lamp for melting carving wax
- Casting flask (contains the investment while it is heated and also the metal is cast into it the flask)
- Rubber sprue base
- Investment
- Rubber mixing bowl
- Centrifugal casting machine
- Flask for metal
- Casting metal, sterling casting grains used
- Flux
- Torch
- Burnout kiln

Here's How

See the *Lost Wax Casting* lesson in the *Techniques* chapter for more information on the lost wax casting method.

Create the Wax Model

1. The leaf design is created by dripping soft wax onto a real dried leaf. First, warm the wax over the alcohol lamp. Drop enough wax onto the leaf for the size needed for the design (see photo 1).

2. Use one of the carving tools with a flat face to smooth the molten wax over the leaf (see photo 2) and build up the surface to a sufficient thickness for whatever application you choose. In this case, I have made a belt buckle.

3. Allow the wax to cool and peel the impression up from the leaf.

4. Add wax shapes to the back of the wax buckle shape to represent the findings of your choice. In this case I added a wax shape like a *staple* for attaching the end of a belt. I also added a prong shape to go through the hole in the belt.

5. Add a sprue to the leaf shape. This will be the channel that the metal flows through to get to the leaf.

Photo 1

Photo 2

Photo 3

6. Attach the sprue to the rubber flask base, smoothing out the transition between the sprue and the base so that it creates a smooth funnel-like transition between the two.

7. Place the flask over the rubber base. Mix and pour the investment into the flask (see photo 3). Allow to set up and dry.

8. Use the kiln to burn out the wax from the mold.

9. Crank the centrifuge three to five times and set the pin so that when released it will spin.

10. Put the metal casting grains into the crucible and melt the metal with the torch. Pull the pin and allow the centrifuge to spin until it stops. The metal will enter the mold as the centrifuge spins. Allow to cool and remove the flask from the centrifuge.

11. Using tongs, hold the flask horizontally and plunge into a large bucket of water until the flask has cooled. Remove the cast metal piece from the water. Dispose of investment and water properly.

Glossary

Abrasives
Any natural or synthetic material used to smooth or polish a surface. Emery paper is a common abrasive used to refine surfaces of metal. Polishing also uses very fine abrasives to further refine the surface and give metal a reflective, shiny surface.

Annealing
The process of heating metal to soften it prior to working. Metal that has been rolled, drawn, hammered, or bent to a work-hardened state can be softened by annealing.

Bench Pin
This is a block of wood with a V-shaped notch that is attached to a work bench and used to brace work while filing and sawing.

Bezel
A bezel is a very thin vertical metal wall surrounding a gemstone or object, used to hold it in place.

Burn Out
A term used in metal casting. It is the process of heating a flask containing investment in a kiln to remove the wax model and prepare it to receive metal for casting.

Buffing/Polishing
Rubbing a metal surface with very fine abrasives to create a reflective shiny surface.

Cross Peen Hammer
A hammer with a wedge shaped profile used to forge and texture metal.

Cuttlefish
A squid-like marine animal with a finely textured calcium rich bony skeleton into which molten metal can be cast.

Findings
A general term used to describe manufactured mechanisms added to jewelry. This includes, but is not limited to ear wires, earring studs, pin clasps, hinges, and chains.

Fire Scale
An oxidized layer of copper produced when metal is heated. Sterling silver, brass, nickel silver, and some gold alloys that contain copper will show this pink or purplish discoloration that must be removed with abrasives.

Flexible Shaft
A machine much like a drill, with a motor and a flexible rotating shaft attached to a hand piece which is controlled by a foot rheostat. Drill bits, burs, texturing and polishing tools are just a sampling of the many instruments available for use with the flex shaft.

Flux
A compound, usually borax based, used to prevent oxides from building up during soldering operations.

Forging
Forming metal by hammering to stretch or shape it.

Fusing
Joining metals by melting at very high temperatures without the use of solder.

Investment
A white plaster-like substance used to surround wax models and contain molten metal in the lost wax casting process.

Karat/Carat
A unit indicating the proportion of pure gold in an alloy. One karat is equal to $1/24$ parts pure gold. 18 karat is $18/24$ pure gold or 75% pure gold with the balance made up of other metals.

Liver of Sulfur
This is also known as potassium sulfide. This yellow compound is mixed with water to create a solution used to darken copper and sterling silver, adding a quick patina to the metal. It smells like rotten eggs and should be used with plenty of ventilation.

Lost Wax Casting
The process of casting metal into a void created with a wax model. Both the wax model and the mold material are destroyed in the casting process.

Mallet
A leather, wood or plastic hammer-like tool which is used to form metal without leaving distinct hammer marks.

Mandrel
A tool usually made of steel or iron, against which metal is hammered. Common tools include ring and bracelet mandrels.

Patina
Coloration of metal through natural or artificial means.

Pierce
Cutting an interior shape into a piece of metal.

Pickle
A mild acid solution used to remove flux and oxides on metal.

Planishing
A process of hammering metal with highly polished hammers to smooth the surface of metal.

Raising
Creating hollow shaped pieces of metal by forming over stakes with the use of hammers and mallets.

Reticulation
A random, textured surface produced on metal by a specific heating process.

Rolling Mill
A machine with steel rolls used to reduce the thickness of sheet metal and wire. It can also be used to make impressions on metal by putting the metal through the mill with a textured object on top of the metal.

Rubber Mold
A flexible mold made from a metal original. Hot wax is injected into the mold to produce multiple models for the lost wax casting process.

Solder
Noun—a metal alloy with a melting point lower than that of its parent material, used to join metal with heat.
Verb—joining metal parts together using heat and metal alloy.

Sprue
Channels through which molten metal flows during the casting process.

Stake
Solid iron, steel, or nylon tools over which metal is formed with the use of mallets or hammers in a process known as raising.

Stamping
Designs and impressions created in metal with the use of metal punches, stamps, or chasing tools.

Work Hardening
The toughening of metal by bending, compressing, drawing, hammering, stretching and rolling, which renders it in a less pliable state.

Metric Conversion Chart

Inches to Millimeters and Centimeters

Inches	MM	CM	Inches	MM	CM
1/8	3	0.3	2	51	5.1
1/4	6	0.6	3	76	7.6
3/8	10	1.0	4	102	10.2
1/2	13	1.3	5	127	12.7
5/8	16	1.6	6	152	15.2
3/4	19	1.9	7	178	17.8
7/8	22	2.2	8	203	20.3
1	25	2.5	9	229	22.9
1 1/4	32	3.2	10	254	25.4
1 1/2	38	3.8	11	279	27.9
1 3/4	44	4.4	12	305	30.5

Index

Index